C000141795

/3

Y Touring Theatre Company presents

Every Breath
by Judith Johnson

Every Breath first toured to London Schools
between 3 March and 11 April 2006

Y Touring Theatre Company is an operation of Central YMCA
Registered charity no. 213121

Every Breath
by Judith Johnson

Anita Katie Donnison
Lina Kate Reynolds
Raz Darren Saul
Sonny Ben Simpson

Director Nigel Townsend
Designer Ben Dickens
Sound Designer Sarah Weltman
Company Manager/Facilitator Thom Hammond
Education Materials Suzi Fowler/Nigel Townsend

For Y Touring Theatre Company
Artistic Director Nigel Townsend
General Manager Michael White
Tour Producer/Administrator Martin Ball

Y Touring Theatre Company would like to thank:
Dr Sophie Petit-Zeman, Dr Jarrod Bailey, Alistair Currie,
Vicky Cowell, Dr Penny Hawkins, Betty McBride,
Professor John Martin, Dr Janet Radcliffe-Richards,
Harald Schmidt.

Photography Bob Workman

Y Touring Theatre Company, c/o Central YMCA
112 Great Russell Street, London WC1B 3NQ
Tel: 0870 1127644

email: info@ytouring.org.uk
www.ytouring.org.uk www.geneticfutures.com

This project was supported by

amrc
representing the charity sector in medical & health research

wellcometrust

Foreword

For almost two decades, Y Touring has been using exceptionally high quality drama to create an open arena for informed debate. Working mainly but not exclusively with young audiences, their projects tackle important, difficult topics, from the ethics of brain research to GM food, animal-to-human transplant to genetic selection, sexuality to bullying. And the list goes on.

Ten years ago, I worked with them on a play called *Cracked*, which challenged the many misconceptions surrounding mental illness. At first, I was sceptical: happy to help, but unsure that theatre could tackle such a complex subject. On seeing that the project really engaged, opened minds, and shifted audiences strikingly away from negative perceptions of those in mental distress, I became convinced of Y Touring's unique skills. The eminent biologist and commentator Professor Lewis Wolpert described their work as 'Theatre of science at its best'.

In 2005, what more exciting challenge, then, than to work with Y Touring to raise the debate, indeed, to raise the level of the debate, about the use of animals in medical research? A time when extremism was capturing headlines, and sensible dialogue risked being stifled in a climate of fear. Starting from the absolute rejection of violent protest, Y Touring brought together people with diverse, sometimes vehemently opposed views, to inform the playwright, Judith Johnson. And, in time, this panel agreed that her provocative, by turns emotional and witty play paints a balanced picture.

Every Breath is captivating school audiences, supported by a suite of educational resources, and will soon be played out for adults too. Yet again, Y Touring's work is stimulating people to think 'in-the-round'. It is testament to the abilities of the entire company that they have fostered the creation of powerful words, and then turned these into compelling theatre.

Life is complicated. Encouraging people to reflect on its toughest questions needs to be rooted in the belief that you can't tell people what to think – and, on the whole, nor should you try – but that enabling and enthusing them to do so brings individual fulfilment within a more understanding society.

Dr Sophie Petit-Zeman
Director of Public Dialogue,
Association of Medical Research Charities
London, March 2006

Writer

Judith Johnson

Judith's plays include *Uganda* for the Royal National Studio/Royal Court (winner of the Thames Best Play Award), *Somewhere* for the Royal National Theatre/ Liverpool Playhouse (winner of a Liverpool Arts Award) and *Shellfish* (English Touring Theatre). TV work includes *Grange Hill*, *The Bill* and *First Sex* (which was nominated for a children's BAFTA). She has also written a number of plays for radio. Her stage plays *The Singing Group* and *Exclude Me* were produced at the Chelsea Theatre to great acclaim, and she was dramaturg for the hit show *Come Out Eli* at the Arcola Theatre. Her musical *Release the Beat*, written with composer Karl Lewcowicz, was also produced at the Arcola. She has written two plays for the Connections Scheme at The National and has now written four plays for Y Touring. *Connected* and *Dear Dilemma* both looked at issues of teenage pregnancy, and *Double the Trouble* explored the difficulties of parenting. *Every Breath* is Judith's first science-based play for the company. She is currently working on a film script, two radio plays and two stage plays.

Cast

Katie Donnison Anita

Theatre: *Exclude Me* (Chelsea Theatre), *Strange Lands* (Courtyard Theatre), *The Suicide Man* (Covent Garden Theatre Museum), *Fine Pair* (Hampstead Theatre Start Night). Television and Film: *The Politician's Wife* (Channel 4), *The Demon Headmaster* (BBC), *Goodnight Sweetheart*, *Casualty*, *Bramwell*, *Bill's New Flock*, *July Wakes*. Voiceover and Radio: *Exclude Me* (BBC Radio Drama), *Angels and Insects*, *The Practical Heart*.

Kate Reynolds Lina

Kate has been a professional actor since the age of twelve. This is her third appearance for Y Touring. Television credits include: *Wycliffe, The Bill, Thing Called Love, Doctors, City Central.*

Darren Saul Raz

Theatre: *We Love Gary*, *My Friend Willy*, *Where's Your Head At*, *Last Days of the Empire*, *Down Dog*, *Common Thread*. Television: *Grange Hill*, *Minder*, *Animal Ark*, *Birds of a Feather*, *A Line in the Sand*, *Judge John Deed*, *The Bill*, *Casualty*, *Holby City*, *Family Affairs*. Film: *Revolution*, *Oxelosund*, *Breathtaking*. Radio: *King Trash*.

Ben Simpson Sonny

Ben is originally from the west country where he started working in professional theatre from a young age. His career has included working in film and television and he has recently finished a year's touring with the Westcountry Theatre Company. Theatre: *The Taming of the Shrew*, *Macbeth*, *Much Ado About Nothing*, *Love Bites*, *Oh Yes You Can* (all Westcountry Theatre Company), *A Christmas*

Carol (the Barbican), *The Sound of Music* (Theatre Royal, Plymouth), *Oliver!* (the Plaza, Exeter and the Octagon, Yeovil). Television: *Holby City*, *The Cazalets*, *The Bill*, *The Phoenix and the Carpet*, *The Treasure Seekers*, *Princess in Love*.

Thom Hammond Company Manager/Facilitator

Thom trained as an actor at ALRA (The Academy of Live & Recorded Artists). *Every Breath* is Thom's fifth tour as Company Manager for Y Touring. Training credits: *Romeo and Juliet* (Mercutio), *The Mill on the Floss* (Stephen Guest), *The Ghost Train* (Teddy Deakin) and *Amadeus* (Antonio Salieri). He represented ALRA in competition for the Laurence Olivier Bursaries and the Carleton Hobbs Awards for BBC Radio Drama. Professional credits: *The Life of Galileo* (BAC), *Richard II* (Young Vic Studio), *Female Transport* (Captive Audience), *Willoughby & Son* (BBC Radio) and *Nathan Barley* (Channel Four).

Company

Nigel Townsend Director

1973–89: Actor, playwright and director for theatre companies including Coventry Belgrade TIE, Humberside Theatre, Cockpit, Greenwich YPT, Young Vic, Battersea Arts, The Unicorn, BBC.

1989–2006: Founder and Artistic Director of Y Touring Theatre Company. For Y Touring Nigel has directed 33 national tours reaching over two million young people, teachers, youth leaders, health and science professionals and members of the general public. Exploring areas such as HIV/AIDS, teenage pregnancy, drug abuse, binge drinking, xenotransplantation, clinical depression, the ethics of brain research, eugenics, stem cell therapy and parenting. Productions include: *Mind the Gap* by Abi Bown; *Headstone* by Rhiannon Tise; *The Inner Circle* by Patricia Loughrey; *Memory Box* by Pete Johnson; *Breathless* by Andrew Alty; *My Friend Willy* by Robert Rigby; *Dear DD* by Judith Johnson; *Connected* by Judith Johnson; *Double the Trouble* by Judith Johnson; *The Gift* by Nicola Baldwin; *Cracked* by Nicola Baldwin; *Wicked Problems* by Nicola Baldwin; *Pig in the Middle* by Judy Upton; *Sweet as You Are* by Jonathan Hall; *Learning to Love the Grey* by Jonathan Hall; *Juggling Chainsaws* by Jonathan Hall; *Coffee Lover's Guide to America* by Jonathan Hall; *Playing God* by Rhiannon Tise; *Where's Your Head At* by Rhiannon Tise; *Wasted* by Rhiannon Tise; *Cell Mates* by Sara Clifford; *The Diagnosis* by Steve Waters.

In 2003 Nigel was responsible for the launch of an innovative new website Genetic Futures (www.geneticfutures.com), and developed a pilot training course for science teachers.

Ben Dickens Designer

Ben has designed seven shows for Y Touring Theatre Company. Theatre work includes a new version of *Peter Pan* that premiered in Sydney for Jim Henson's creature shop, and a Noël Coward double bill for the West End. Ben has recently designed two touring shows for the BBC, *Balamory* and *Fireman Sam*, and is currently designing a new show for Channel Five. Film and television work includes *28 Days Later*, *The Libertine*, *Waking the Dead* and *Lenny Blue*.

Sarah Weltman Sound Designer

Sarah's recent sound designs include *The Mouse Queen* (New Victory Theatre, New York); for Mama Quillo Productions – *Bones* (Leicester Haymarket) and *Bites* (The Bush Theatre); *Over Gardens Out* (Southwark Playhouse); *Bread and Butter* (Tricycle Theatre); for the Young Vic Theatre – *Six Characters Looking for an Author, A Night at the Circus* (PUSH), *Red Demon,* and as part of Direct Action Season *Winners, Interior, The Exception and the Rule* and *The New Tenant*; for Y Touring – *Headstone* (Arcola Theatre), *Mind the Gap, The Gift, Wasted* and *Pig In The Middle*; *Mr Elliot* (Chelsea Theatre); *The BFG, How the Other Half Loves, The Ugly Duckling, Driving Miss Daisy, American Buffalo* (Dukes Playhouse, Lancaster).

Suzi Fowler Education Materials

Suzi studied Drama at Aberystwyth University before working as a Drama Teacher at a Secondary School in Reading. In 1999 she joined Riding Lights Theatre Company, York, initially as an actor and later as Education Officer where she set up and ran Education Projects with local schools and Riding Lights Youth Theatre. Theatre credits include: *The Time of Your Life* (1999/2000 Riding Lights Roughshod), *The Christmas Conspiracy* (1999 Riding Lights Roughshod), *Friendly Fire* (2000 Riding Lights), *Science Friction* (2004 Riding Lights Schools Tour), *Invisible Ink* (Riding Lights Schools Tour).

Michael White General Manager

Michael has worked in many London theatre venues and for a diverse range of theatre, live art practitioners, photography, dance and installation artists which have toured nationally and internationally. Previous production credits include *Civil, Finale, Three Duets, Audiology* (for Pacitti Company); *Peeling, The Trouble with Richard* (for Graeae Theatre Company); *Nightbird '02, C'est Vauxhall* (for Duckie); *Jewess Tattooess* (for Marissa Carnesky); *Animal, Hoxton Story* (for the Red Room).

Martin Ball Tour Producer/Administrator

Previous production credits include *Non-Sexual Kissing* (2003 National Tour and Pleasance Edinburgh) and *Beyond a Joke* (2004 National Tour and Pleasance Edinburgh) for the Cambridge Footlights, *Luke & Stella* (Canal Café and Pleasance Edinburgh), *Cowards* (Hen and Chickens and Pleasance Edinburgh) and *Alex Horne: When in Rome* (Hen and Chickens and Pleasance Edinburgh) for Bound and Gagged Comedy and *Back In Town Again* (Underbelly Edinburgh and National Tour) and *Diagnosis* (Hen and Chickens) for Jonny Grommitts Productions/CUADC. Martin studied History at Cambridge University, graduating in July 2005.

 touring

Y Touring Theatre Company

Y Touring Theatre Company exists to promote healthy citizenship and healthy communities through the creation of theatre, drama and new media programmes that allow our audiences to engage with a wide variety of contemporary cultural, social, moral and spiritual concerns; deal with universal themes; provide the opportunity to observe the dynamics of human relationships; show the possibility of change; prioritise the education of the emotions; offer approaches to sensitive issues, especially in response to new knowledge; and encourage questioning, analysis and debate.

> **'Ways of engaging the public in debate on scientific issues, like the applications of genetic technology, are desperately needed. The way not to do it is for the media to provide images of scientists and their creations as monsters. But a highly imaginative theatrical venture by Y Touring Theatre Company may have found a brilliant solution.'**
> PROF LEWIS WOLPERT, *THE INDEPENDENT*

Y Touring Theatre Company was established in 1989 as an operation of Central YMCA. Y Touring is widely recognised as one of the UK's leading young people's companies.

The operation produces shows that tour the UK and internationally to an audience of young people and adults.

The operation's work has focused on using theatre and drama to explore health and science and society. The touring programmes consist of a play by a leading contemporary dramatist followed by an audience debate. Extensive online resources support all programmes. These are designed to enable teachers and students to further their understanding of the issues explored.

> **'Y Touring has shown that theatre can be a powerful tool for the communication of science to a wide audience.'**
> PROF COLIN BLAKEMORE, Professor of Physiology,
> University of Oxford, President of the British Association and
> Director of the Oxford Centre for Cognitive Neuroscience

Since the operation was formed the company has reached over two million young people in the UK. Works have tackled a wide range of issues including grief and loss, teenage pregnancy, sex and relationships, mental illness, parenting, immigration, sexuality, stem cell therapy, Alzheimer's disease, 'designer babies' and xenotransplantation (animal-to-human organ transplants). Y Touring also runs a youth theatre, has produced an interactive educational film on genetic selection and has produced four scripts written especially for large groups of young people available through the internet from the National Theatre Bookshop.

www.ytouring.org.uk
www.geneticfutures.com
info@ytouring.org.uk

EVERY BREATH

First published in 2006 by Oberon Books Ltd
521 Caledonian Road, London N7 9RH
Tel: 020 7607 3637 / Fax: 020 7607 3629
e-mail: info@oberonbooks.com
www.oberonbooks.com

Characters

ANITA
21 years old, a science graduate, about to do her PhD.

SONNY
Her brother, 18. Just finished his A-Levels.

LINA
Sonny and Anita's mum. 40-something.
Works at a garden centre.

RAZ
Late thirties/early forties. Painter and decorator.
Trying to have a relationship with Lina.

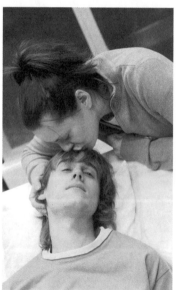

Photographs from the production
Clockwise, from top left: Anita (Katie Donnison), Sonny (Ben Simpson);
Raz (Darren Saul), Anita; Raz, Lina (Kate Reynolds); Lina, Sonny.

Photographs by Bob Workman

Scene 1: SONNY's bedroom

Posters of bands and music festivals on the walls. SONNY is into indie music. At the moment though, he's sitting on his bed reading an animal rights magazine. We can't see the cover so don't know what kind of mag it is. He is also listening to music on his iPod or Discman. He has a look of disgust on his face. Enter LINA.

LINA: Sonny?

No answer. SONNY is transfixed.

Sonny?

Still no answer. LINA looks at the magazine over his shoulder. She flinches, looks shocked.

What's that?!!

SONNY turns and sees his mum. Scrambles his headphones off. Hides the mag under his pillow.

SONNY: You weren't meant to see that.

LINA: What on earth was it?

SONNY: Dogs.

LINA: Dogs!!

SONNY: Beagles. I'm sorry Mum. They're experiment dogs. It's horrible.

Beat.

LINA: Most boys your age sneak off to read different types of magazines!

SONNY: Not me.

LINA ruffles his hair.

I use the internet for that sort of thing.

LINA: Sonny!

She gets the mag from under his pillow.

What are they, smoking beagles?

SONNY: No! That was in the 70s, they don't test cigarettes on animals anymore in this country. You're showing your age now.

LINA: Thank you darling.

SONNY: It's a farm. They breed dogs there. The conditions they keep them in look really bad.

LINA: You sure? I thought they had rules and regulations for that sort of thing.

SONNY: They have, but that doesn't mean people stick to them.

LINA: (*Taking mag.*) Where did you get this from?

SONNY: (*Taking it back.*) Animal Kind. Kelsey took me to a meeting last night.

LINA: (*Suggestively.*) Kelsey eh?

SONNY: She's just a friend mother. (*Looking at mag.*) The female dogs have litter after litter after litter of puppies, they're just breeding machines. And when they stop producing enough puppies they kill them and use their blood and stuff for more experiments.

LINA: That's a shame love.

SONNY: 'That's a shame love.' You always say something like that.

LINA: No I don't!

SONNY: Yes you do. If something controversial comes up. You just sit on the fence.

LINA: What d'you want me to do? I'd go and rescue the puppies right now, but then who would cook your tea?

SONNY: You wouldn't rescue them, you don't even like animals.

LINA: (*Sighs. They've been through this before.*) I do like animals, I just don't have the time to look after any.

SONNY pulls tongues at her. She pulls tongues back.

SONNY: Oh. Listen. Kelsey's invited me to a protest on Wednesday night. Outside this new animal research laboratory they're trying to build in town.

LINA: (*Worried.*) Sonny.

SONNY: It's a peaceful protest. Don't worry.

LINA: Some of these animal rights people are really violent.

SONNY: (*Sighs.*) Hardly any of them are like that, that's just the media trying to sensationalise things. The people I met at Animal Kind are really peaceful, they're just against suffering. There's a lot of women your age!

LINA: Oh well then. Nothing exciting there.

Pause. LINA lingers, she rocks back and forward on her heels.

SONNY: What?

LINA: What d'you mean what?

SONNY: You're doing that thing.

LINA: (*Doing it.*) What thing?

SONNY: Rocking. Like a policeman. It means you want to say something.

LINA: Oh.

Another pause. More rocking.

SONNY: Mum!

LINA: I've, em, I've invited someone. For dinner. On Saturday.

SONNY: (*Beat.*) Someone?

LINA: It's a man.

SONNY: (*Clasping his chest.*) Oh my God, a man!!

LINA: (*Hits him.*) Stop it!

SONNY: (*Faking a heart attack, putting on a voice.*) 'No no, I will not see him. You must not have a life of your own!'

LINA: Don't!

SONNY's pretend attack goes into a small fit of real coughing. He quickly recovers.

Where's your inhaler?

SONNY: Er, downstairs. I'm alright. So go on then.

LINA: Go on what?

SONNY: What's his name? How old is he?

LINA: His name's Raz and he's 39.

SONNY: Raz?

LINA: Yes!

SONNY: So. Is he blind, or has he just come out of prison and he's desperate?

LINA: Oi!

LINA gives SONNY a kick. He throws a pillow at her. She picks up a book and throws it at him, hard. It hits him.

SONNY: Ow!

LINA: Don't take the mickey! He's a painter and decorator actually.

SONNY: And?

LINA: And what?

SONNY: More details!

LINA: I met him when he was painting the fences at the garden centre. I think you'll like him. He's a really interesting guy. You will make sure you're here won't you?

SONNY: I wouldn't miss it for the world. I'm working on the Pussy Cat Van on Saturday but I'm sure I'll be back by then.

Beat.

LINA: (*Amused.*) You're working where?

SONNY: The Pussy Cat Van. The cat rescue minibus. Kelsey's driving, I'm going to help handle the cats.

LINA: What cats?

SONNY: We're rescuing stray cats, and pet cats that people don't want anymore.

LINA: You're spending a lot of time with this Kelsey. For someone who's 'just a friend'.

SONNY: We've got a lot in common. (*Beat.*) Er, Mum.

LINA: (*Knows what he's going to ask.*) No.

SONNY: Look, I'm 18, I'd look after it myself.

LINA: You're not having a cat.

SONNY: You're really mean. You've never let us have a pet.

LINA: We both know that I'd end up looking after it.

SONNY: You wouldn't!

LINA: Oh yeah? So what you gonna do with it when you go to Uni? They allow cats in the Halls of Residence do they?

SONNY: (*Sighs.*) Alright.

LINA: Right. I'm gonna make tea.

She goes to exit then remembers something.

Oh, by the way. Your sister's coming home too. For dinner, on Saturday.

SONNY: (*Not impressed.*) Oh great.

LINA: I don't want any arguing from you two. Okay? I want a truce. I don't want Raz thinking he's entered a war zone.

SONNY: I'll try. I can't speak for her.

LINA: I've spoken to her and she's promised to behave if you do.

SONNY: (*Sarky.*) Why not do a star chart Mum? Like when we were kids. If we get through dinner without arguing you can buy us both a treat. (*An idea.*) Actually, no, you can let me have a cat!

LINA: Please Sonny. It's important to me.

Beat.

SONNY: (*Sincere.*) Alright Mum. I'll do my best.

LINA smiles. Nods. Goes to exit.

Mum?

LINA: Yeah?

SONNY: Don't wear your lycra trousers. Okay?

LINA laughs. She picks another book up and chucks it at him. This time, SONNY catches it.

Hah!

They exit. End of scene.

Scene 2: Garden centre

LINA is wearing a garden centre tunic and potting up a plant. After a moment, RAZ comes in. He is wearing a very lairy T-shirt with a daft slogan on ('I am the weakest link. Hello!' springs to mind). Either way it isn't cool. He is carrying a wrapped-up present.

LINA: (*Looks up, surprised.*) Hello!

RAZ: Hi there.

LINA goes to RAZ, she goes to kiss him awkwardly on the cheek. He goes for the lips. They both miss and bash noses.

LINA / RAZ: Sorry! / Whoops!

RAZ: (*Rubbing his nose.*) Shall we try that again?

LINA: Er, Let's not.

Slight pause.

(*Ironic.*) Nice T-Shirt!

RAZ: Thanks! (*Ironic back.*) I like to keep up with fashion.

LINA: Yes. I've noticed that about you.

RAZ: I brought you a present.

LINA: Are we, meant to be... [meeting?]

RAZ: (*Cutting in.*) No, I was passing. (*Re present:*) 'I saw this and I thought of you.'

LINA: (*Taking present.*) Aw! Thank you!

RAZ: And, you know, it's nearly lunch time so...

LINA: Oh, I'm on a late lunch today!

RAZ: Ah. Never mind. You gonna open that?

LINA: Oh, yes.

She unwraps the present. It's a book. 'Buddhism for Beginners'.

RAZ: It's the one I was telling you about.

LINA: 'An Introduction to Buddhism.'

RAZ: It's short with big letters. Even I understood it!

LINA: Thank you, I'll look forward to reading it.

Slightly awkward pause.

RAZ: I'm sorry. I've taken you a bit by surprise haven't I?
It's just that I was passing and…

LINA: No! Not at all. (*Gabbling.*) I'm just… I'm not very
good at…being spontaneous. My kids tell me I'm really
boring, but I think I've just got used to everything being
planned you know, being a single parent, everything
always has to run like clockwork, so… Oh listen to me,
wittering on!

RAZ: I wish I was a bit more organised.

LINA: Just, you know, they had to get to school and I had
to get to work, we had such definite routines. It's weird
to think they're all grown up now, I don't have to…
Oh I'm wittering again, all I mean is I'm not used to
surprises, but it's very nice to see you anyway!

RAZ: Thank you. Did you tell your kids I'm coming on
Saturday?

LINA: Yeah.

RAZ: How did that go?

LINA: Fine actually. Sonny was fine anyway. Anita was a
bit cool but that's Anita for you. Cool as a cucumber.
Until she loses her temper, then she's sharp as a knife.

RAZ: I'd better stay on the right side of her then.

LINA: Yeah.

RAZ: Did you tell them anything about me?

LINA: Not very much. I said you were interesting.

RAZ: (*Pleased.*) Interesting am I?

LINA: I think so.

RAZ: Uneducated, unskilled, ex-punk?

LINA: You're not unskilled. You did a great job on our fences.

RAZ: Yeah they did turn out pretty good.

LINA: I think my boss is going to give you some more work.

RAZ: Oh yeah?

LINA: She wants to refit the indoor plants shelving.

RAZ: Smashing.

Pause.

LINA: I'm quite nervous about Saturday.

RAZ: You're nervous!

LINA: They're quite…lively, my kids.

RAZ: Lively's good.

LINA: Depends what kind of lively it is. They don't…

Beat.

RAZ: Don't what?

LINA: They don't always get on very well.

RAZ: Do any brothers and sisters?

LINA: I kind of hoped they'd have grown out of it by now. Anita's nearly 22!

RAZ: Family rows are just normal aren't they? Don't worry about it.

LINA: I'll…try not to.

Pause. LINA looks worried.

RAZ: What're we having to eat?

LINA: It's going to be vegetarian because of Sonny.

RAZ: Oh good, I'm thinking of going veggie myself.

LINA: Are you?

RAZ: Yeah. You know, if I'm gonna go down the Buddhist track.

LINA: Are all Buddhists vegetarians?

RAZ: I don't think so. But it is recommended. Because of, you know, not wanting to hurt other living things.

LINA: Oh! So you and Sonny'll have a lot in common!

RAZ: Although I do love a nice big steak from time to time. Steak and chips with fried tomato. S'gonna be hard giving that sort of thing up. If I do go down that road.

LINA: D'you think you will?

RAZ: I'm finding the meditation a bit hard going.

LINA: Yes, I think I would.

RAZ: I can do ten minutes sitting still, but forty. It's a bit steep.

LINA: Forty?

RAZ: Yeah. Supposed to do it every day. I keep getting cramp in me buttocks.

LINA: (*Laughs.*) In your where?

RAZ: Me buttocks. (*Laughing.*) Don't laugh. You try sitting cross-legged on a little stool for forty minutes!

LINA: Maybe you should try a shorter time, build up to forty?

RAZ: Maybe I should. Is your daughter veggie too?

LINA: Oh no! Not that one. She's a total carnivore. But I thought I'd cook veggie for us all on Saturday, just to make it easier. She'll just have to put up with it.

RAZ: Yeah.

Awkward pause.

LINA: Listen, I'd…better get on.

RAZ: Oh! Yeah. Okay.

LINA: Thanks again. For the book. It was lovely to see you.

They go to kiss again, this time a bit more successfully and on the lips.

RAZ: Yes! Right on target.

LINA: Sorry?

RAZ: Er, nothing. I'll see you Saturday.

He exits. LINA watches him go, smiling. End of scene.

Scene 3: LINA's kitchen, Saturday morning

SONNY is reading (music paper – NME?) and eating a bowl of healthy-looking breakfast: muesli with chopped fruit on top. He's wearing a 'Pussy Cat Van' T-shirt. It's a few sizes too big for him. After a moment, ANITA comes in. She's carrying a small holdall. SONNY turns round and sees her. He goes back to eating his muesli.

SONNY: You're early.

ANITA: I got an early train. We don't all lie in bed until lunchtime little bro.

SONNY: (*Looks around.*) Hello? It's ten o'clock? Is this my bedroom? And don't call me little bro!

ANITA: You look like you're still wearing your pyjamas.

SONNY: No I don't.

ANITA: (*Peering at SONNY's T-shirt, reading.*) The Pussy Cat Van!

She starts laughing.

SONNY: Shut up.

ANITA: The Pussy Cat Van! What is that? One of those weird bands you like?

SONNY: It's a cat rescue organisation. Not that you'd care.

ANITA: Poor ickle pussy cats! Are these people still at Nursery School? Why don't they call animals by their proper names?

SONNY gets up to put his now empty bowl in the sink. The bagginess of his shirt becomes even more apparent.

And why don't they give their volunteers the right sized shirts?

SONNY: The guy before me was big, okay? It's a charity. They don't have enough money to keep buying T-shirts.

ANITA: Poor ickle pussy wussy charitypies.

SONNY: Shut up.

ANITA: Where's Mum?

SONNY: She's gone to the supermarket.

ANITA: Already?

SONNY: I think she's nervous about this meal.

ANITA: Brilliant! I can't wait. Hopefully she'll get drunk and start singing Kylie songs like she does at Christmas. Has she told you anything about this guy?

SONNY: His name's Raz.

ANITA: I know. I thought he was a teenager when she first told me.

SONNY: She said he's really interesting.

ANITA: As long as he can string a sentence together.

SONNY: I don't know if he'll be able to converse on your level. Einstein.

ANITA: What d'you mean my level? I can talk to anyone.

SONNY: Oh yeah? I thought they had to have at least three A-Levels before they could be your friend.

ANITA: I was 12 when I said that.

SONNY: At least I qualify now.

ANITA: Oh yes! I forgot. Congratulations are in order.

SONNY: (*Bashful.*) I didn't get straight As like you… [did]

ANITA: (*Cutting in.*) I hear you're going to do (*Bit of attitude.*) 'Enviromental Studies'.

SONNY: That's right.

ANITA: (*Sneering a bit.*) Global warming and all that? Hoping to save the world are we?

SONNY: It's not just about global warming.

ANITA: I thought you wanted to be a vet.

SONNY: Yes. Well. I couldn't quite manage the grades. I didn't stay in for two years every night with my head stuck in a school book. I have friends and a social life.

ANITA: I've got friends.

SONNY: Yeah. More boffins like yourself. What do you talk about? Scientific formulas?

ANITA: 'Boffins'. Grow up little bro.

SONNY: (*Getting impatient.*) Look Anita, you do your thing, I'll do mine, okay.

ANITA: (*Coolly.*) Fine by me.

Pause. ANITA starts looking for food.

Anything for breakfast?

SONNY: When Mum gets back. There's muesli.

ANITA: Bunny food. I fancy a nice fry up.

SONNY: I'm going.

ANITA: Have fun with the pussy wussys.

SONNY: Piss off.

SONNY goes to exit. As he does so he starts coughing. It goes on a bit longer than usual. ANITA looks a bit worried.

ANITA: Where's your inhaler?

SONNY: (*Through coughs.*) I've ditched it.

ANITA: You've what?

SONNY: (*Recovering.*) I…don't want to use it anymore.

ANITA: Sonny!

SONNY: It's okay. I haven't had an attack for years. I don't need it anymore.

ANITA: What does the doctor have to say about this?

SONNY: I haven't spoken to the doctor, I…

ANITA: What? What does Mum think?

SONNY: I haven't told her either, I've…

ANITA: Oh great.

SONNY: I've got it under control. I'm eating an anti-asthma diet and I've been taking magnesium and doing breathing exercises.

ANITA: I don't believe this. Are you still taking the steroids?

SONNY: No.

ANITA: Sonny!

SONNY: Look, they researched them using animals.

ANITA: What?!! What difference does that make?

SONNY: A lot of difference. I don't want to take anything that's been researched or tested on animals.

ANITA: Where's this come from?!

SONNY: I don't want to add anymore to the vast profits these pharmaceutical companies are making, and I don't want animals to suffer because of me.

ANITA: Oh great, brilliant. How clever of you! How many A-Levels did you say you got? All medicines are tested on animals. It's against the law not to test them!

SONNY: I've got to go now. Promise me you won't tell Mum.

ANITA: You are an idiot.

SONNY: Promise me. I don't want to worry her.

Pause. ANITA narrows her eyes at him.

ANITA: The only reason I'm not going to tell her today is because I don't want to spoil her special meal. Tomorrow is a different matter.

SONNY: Alright. Alright. See you later.

ANITA: Go on. Go and rescue the fluffy little cattypoos.

SONNY leaves. ANITA watches him go, shaking her head.

Scene 4: LINA's kitchen, evening

LINA is looking in the oven. After a bit, ANITA comes in, reading the book about Buddhism. LINA gets knives and forks out and starts laying the table. She seems very nervous.

ANITA: So, according to this, it's wrong to hurt any living thing. Hah!

LINA: Yes, well, that's right isn't it?

ANITA: You think so mother? What if a man jumped out and tried to attack you one night. Wouldn't you try to fight him off?

LINA: Well, yes, I suppose so.

ANITA: What if a dog had attacked a baby? Wouldn't you shoot it? I know I would.

LINA: Ye-es.

ANITA: What if you were swimming in the sea and a shark was coming towards you with its jaws wide open? And you had a torpedo gun. Wouldn't...

LINA: Yes, I take your point Anita.

ANITA: I mean, animals hurt each other all the time, most of them, they're vicious.

LINA: *(Preoccupied.)* Mm.

ANITA: You can't go through life without hurting things. How many flies have you swatted in your life?

LINA: I try not to darling.

ANITA: Ugh! You let them fly around the house spreading shit all over the place?

LINA: Anita.

LINA opens a bottle of red wine and puts it on the table with four glasses.

SONNY: (*Coming in, wearing Pussy Cat Van T-shirt.*) What time's supper Mum?

ANITA: Five minutes. Where've you been?

SONNY: I'll just go and get changed.

SONNY exits. LINA gets an enormous bowl of salad out and puts it in the middle of the table. She stands and looks at it, rocking back and forwards on her heels.

LINA: D'you think I've made too much salad?

ANITA: We won't go hungry anyway.

LINA: (*Worried.*) No. Maybe I should take some out?

ANITA: Mother. Stop worrying.

LINA: Okay.

ANITA: Has he got a shaved head and love beads?

LINA: What?

ANITA: This Raz. That's what Buddhists look like.

LINA: He's just thinking about becoming a Buddhist.

The doorbell goes.

Oh God. That'll be him.

ANITA: You want me to get it?

LINA: Yes. No! I don't know.

The doorbell goes again. Pause.

I'd better.

ANITA: Okay.

LINA exits. SONNY comes back in, wearing a different T-shirt.

SONNY: (*Whispers.*) Is that him?

ANITA: (*Leaning in, whispering sarcastically.*) I don't know, I can't see through the wall.

SONNY flicks her on the nose. She slaps him on the side of the head. LINA comes in followed by RAZ. SONNY and ANITA jump apart. RAZ is wearing a T-shirt even more lurid and daft than the one in the previous scene. Possibly with the slogan 'I'm only visiting this planet'. LINA is carrying a big bunch of flowers given to her by RAZ.

LINA: So, here we are. Sonny, Anita. This is Raz.

RAZ: Hi Guys!

Silence for a second. SONNY and ANITA stare at RAZ in his T-shirt.

SONNY: Er, hi!

SONNY shakes RAZ' hand.

ANITA: Hello.

ANITA does likewise.

LINA: Look at the lovely flowers Raz brought me!

ANITA: That's a good idea, buying flowers for someone who works in a garden centre.

Beat. LINA throws ANITA a stern look.

Sorry.

RAZ: Ah! But I got these ones from the florists!

ANITA: Ingenious!

RAZ: Thank you.

SONNY: Nice T-shirt Raz.

RAZ: Thank you!

ANITA: Yes, very witty.

RAZ: You think so?

ANITA smirks. A moment of awkwardness.

LINA: I'll, er, put these in some water. The food's nearly ready.

SONNY: I'll do that for you Mum.

SONNY takes the flowers.

LINA: Thanks darling. Why don't you sit down Raz. Would you like a glass of wine?

RAZ: Yes please.

RAZ sits. SONNY deals with the flowers. LINA pours herself and RAZ a glass of wine, and one for ANITA too. ANITA and LINA sit.

Cheers!

ANITA / LINA: Cheers.

RAZ: Here's to…T-shirts!

LINA giggles. ANITA rolls her eyes.

LINA: I'll…get the quiche.

As they talk, LINA goes to get quiche out of the oven and serve it up. SONNY puts flowers on table and sits down, pours himself some wine.

RAZ: So, Anita, I hear you're a real live scientist!

ANITA: That's me!

RAZ: I've never met one in the flesh before.

ANITA: How do you know?

RAZ: Not that I'm aware of.

ANITA: We're everywhere you know. Some of your best friends may be scientists and you wouldn't even know it.

RAZ: Ah, yes! Meeting in secret to conduct dastardly experiments!

SONNY: They do that anyway.

ANITA makes a face at SONNY. LINA gives them all quiche.

LINA: Help yourselves to salad.

They do so. The conversation continues as they eat.

SONNY: Mum was telling me you've done a lot of travelling Raz.

RAZ: Yes. Soon as I left school. Well I say left, asked to leave is more like it.

ANITA: Ooh! Excluded!

RAZ: I think that's what they call it these days. It was more of a mutual agreement between me and the School. I was a bit of a bad lad I'm afraid.

ANITA: Really?

RAZ: I got in with a bad crowd. It was a bit rough, where I lived. Soon as I got the chance I was out of there. Travelling the world!

SONNY: What was your favourite country?

RAZ: Mm. Interesting question. India probably, especially Goa. I got stuck there for three years!

LINA: I bet you did.

RAZ: Don't remember much about it though!

ANITA: (*Mock innocent, taking the piss.*) Oh! Why's that?

RAZ: (*Laughs, looks at LINA.*) Er…

SONNY: Stop it Anita.

ANITA pulls tongues at SONNY. Slight pause. LINA frowns.

RAZ: Lovely quiche Lina!

LINA: Thank you. It's goat's cheese.

SONNY: It's delicious Mum.

ANITA makes a face 'Yuck'.

LINA: More wine anyone?

LINA pours. SONNY coughs a bit. Recovers.

RAZ: I hear you're interested in animal rights Sonny?

SONNY: (*Glancing at ANITA.*) That's right.

ANITA: (*Sneering.*) Animal rights!

RAZ: (*Ignores her.*) Is it the food industry that bothers you? Battery farming, all that stuff?

SONNY: Yes, that. But at the moment, the group I've just joined, we're campaigning against animals being used in medical research.

ANITA exchanges glances with LINA. She sighs and tuts loudly.

RAZ: Ah, yes, quite a lot of suffering there I should imagine.

ANITA: 'Imagine' is right. Neither of you know anything about it.

LINA: Anita.

SONNY: (*To RAZ.*) We've been leafleting in town, about the animal research laboratory actually.

ANITA: (*Sitting up, glancing at LINA.*) Really?

SONNY: (*To RAZ.*) I could give you some information about it if you like.

ANITA: If you like reading unproven propaganda he means.

LINA: Anita. Please.

ANITA: 'Anita. Please.' Why don't you tell him, he's the one talking rubbish.

SONNY: (*To RAZ, ignoring ANITA.*) We're very concerned about the use of primates in brain research.

RAZ: Oh yes?

SONNY: They operate on monkeys. They give them brain damage. It's awful/

ANITA: (*Cutting in.*) This is rubbish. Hardly anyone uses primates. Most of the animals used in scientific procedures are rodents.

SONNY: But they will be using macaque monkeys in the new lab.

ANITA: Yes but…

SONNY: You think it's alright to perform unnecessary operations on defenceless animals who can't say no?

ANITA: Look. If you ever have the misfortune to suffer from a brain disease you'll thank the scientists who've used monkeys for helping you.

SONNY: I'd rather thank the monkeys. How many of them suffered? And died?

ANITA: How many men died in World War Two to stop the Nazis taking over? Would you rather they hadn't?

SONNY: What a ridiculous thing to say! Those men could say no.

LINA: Children.

ANITA: So what if you got leukaemia like Dad?

LINA: (*Sharp.*) Anita!

Beat.

SONNY: I haven't got leukaemia.

ANITA: But what if you got it? Wouldn't you take the drugs because animals were used in the research that developed them?

SONNY: I don't think I would no.

ANITA: Oh great. So you'd rather have seen your Dad suffer even more!

SONNY: I'm not saying that.

ANITA: (*Cutting in.*) You don't even remember. You wouldn't be saying this if you did.

SONNY: (*Cross.*) I do remember!

ANITA: His painkillers were the only thing that kept him sane.

SONNY: Didn't cure him though, did they? All these scientists. How many animals have they used and they still haven't found a cure for cancer.

ANITA: That doesn't mean they shouldn't try!!! Dad would have wanted them to try!

SONNY: Oh yeah, Dad's always on your side isn't he? Even from his grave.

Beat. Awkward silence. LINA looks mortified.

ANITA: (*Taken aback.*) That's not…

LINA: (*Cutting in.*) That's enough.

ANITA: He's not…

LINA: Truce Anita.

ANITA: I…

LINA: TRUCE!!!

Silence. They eat. ANITA looks very angry. SONNY coughs.

I'm sorry Raz.

RAZ: Don't worry.

They eat. Silence. After a moment RAZ tries to re-ignite the conversation.

So. Anita. I hear you're about to do your PhD?

ANITA: (*Still cross.*) Yeah.

RAZ: What is a PhD exactly?

ANITA: (*Sharp.*) Don't you know?

RAZ: I've never been to University myself. (*Attempting a joke.*) 'Part from the 'University of Life' of course.

RAZ laughs. No one else does. LINA squeezes RAZ' hand.

ANITA: (*Impatient.*) It's a research project. You do it when you've finished your degree.

RAZ: What you going to be researching?

ANITA looks at LINA, worried.

ANITA: Er…it's a bit difficult to explain.

RAZ: Go on. If my brain starts hurting I'll let you know.

LINA shakes her head at ANITA, warning her off.

ANITA: Well…

RAZ: Try not to use words with more than two syllables.

ANITA: I'm, er,

ANITA looks at her mum.

LINA: (*Warning.*) Anita.

Beat. SONNY looks up sharply.

SONNY: What?

ANITA: (*To LINA.*) I'll have to tell him some time!

LINA: Not now!

SONNY: What?!!

Beat.

ANITA: I'm going to be working at the new laboratory.

Silence. LINA holds her head in her hands. Beat.

SONNY: (*Quiet anger.*) What are you going to be doing?

ANITA: It's…complicated. We want to examine mice. The way genes work in their hearts and livers at different times of the day.

RAZ: Come again?

SONNY: I don't believe this.

ANITA: The mice will be very well looked after. They have to be healthy or they wouldn't be good to experiment on.

RAZ: What's the experiment for Anita?

ANITA: For?

RAZ: Yeah, are you looking for a cure for something?

ANITA: Er, no. No we're just…studying the mice. To understand more about the genetic make-up of their hearts and livers.

RAZ: Ri-ight.

SONNY: What happens to the mice when you've finished 'studying' them?

ANITA: Well. We, you know, kill them.

SONNY tuts loudly.

That's how we study their genetic make-up. We look at their organs.

SONNY: What a sick waste of life.

ANITA: Mum, can you tell him?

LINA: You are being a bit over-dramatic Sonny! We should be proud of Anita, you never know what she might find out while she's studying her mice. She might be the one who finds the cure for cancer.

SONNY: What? And you're calling me over-dramatic.

LINA: There are examples of scientists stumbling across things while researching something else.

RAZ: I know one! Viagra! I heard about it on the radio. It was actually made to treat heart disease, not get your heart going.

RAZ laughs at his joke. No one else does.

ANITA: Basic research is about acquiring knowledge. It doesn't have to lead to a cure for something.

SONNY: So then why do it if… [it doesn't]

ANITA: (*Overlaps.*) Because we need to know. We need to understand.

SONNY: You don't need to know, you just want to know.

ANITA: (*Dismissive.*) Don't be silly.

SONNY: (*Angry.*) I'm not being… [silly]

LINA: (*Cutting in.*) Look. I'm sure Raz doesn't want to hear anymore of this.

SONNY: But she's… [calling me names]

LINA: (*Cutting in.*) Does anyone want any more salad?

ANITA: (*Deliberately polite.*) I'll have some please Mum.

LINA passes salad to ANITA. She helps herself. SONNY fumes. A moment's awkwardness, then:

(*Falsely cheerful.*) So. I hear you're a painter and decorator Raz.

RAZ: Er yeah. At the moment anyway. Jack of all trades me!

ANITA: What's the best job you've ever done?

RAZ: Mm, let's think. I was a cowboy for a bit in the States.

ANITA: (*Amused.*) A cowboy?

RAZ: Yeah, not for long though. Kept falling off the horse!

LINA, RAZ and ANITA laugh.

SONNY: (*Can't hold it in any longer.*) How will you be killing them?

LINA: Sonny!

SONNY: No, I want to know!

ANITA: Different people use different methods and do we really want to talk about this over dinner?

SONNY: What method will you use?

LINA: Sonny stop it!

ANITA: (*Sighs.*) If you really need to know, I use dislocation of the neck. It's meant to be the quickest way.

SONNY: 'Dislocation'. You break their necks you mean! I don't know how you can do it.

ANITA: I won't enjoy it Sonny!

SONNY: So don't do it!

ANITA: It's a necessary part of the job, life can't all be fluffy little bunnykins hopping through the fields you know!

SONNY: (*Cutting in.*) You just want to go on doing your 'interesting work' like all the other scientists. You don't want to think about the animals because thinking about the animals means you'd have to stop.

ANITA: (*Losing it.*) Oh grow up, you're talking shit now.

SONNY: Oh how scientific.

ANITA: Wait until you're a bit older and a bit less naïve and we'll have this discussion again.

SONNY: Don't patronise me.

ANITA: Don't talk crap then.

SONNY: You've always done that (*He coughs.*) to me.

ANITA: Only when you've deserved it, little bro.

SONNY: You and Dad. Sitting by his bedside with your nose in some book together. 'Oh my daughter, she's so clever.'

LINA: He thought you were clever too!

SONNY: No he didn't. I used to be desperate for him to sit and read with me but he was always too tired. Too ill. He only made the effort for little Miss Brainbox. Even when he wasn't ill he didn't have time for me because I wasn't as quick as she was.

ANITA: That's rubbish.

SONNY starts wheezing.

SONNY: You think you know everything, you think you're so right, but you don't question anything. You think science is all about being definite, about being right. Well this time you're wrong. You're wrong. But your mind's so tight shut, you can't see it.

By the end of this speech SONNY is coughing and wheezing quite a bit.

LINA: Sonny, where's your inhaler?

ANITA: Shit.

SONNY starts having a severe asthma attack.

LINA: (*Running to SONNY.*) Where's your inhaler?!

ANITA: Mum. He hasn't got it.

SONNY is gasping for breath.

LINA: What?

ANITA: He's chucked it away.

RAZ: (*Gets phone out.*) I'll call an ambulance.

LINA: Sonny! Sonny!

SONNY collapses, unconscious. End of scene.

Scene 5: The hospital, next day

SONNY lies in bed asleep. LINA comes in. She is wearing her outdoor coat and has a bag with some stuff for SONNY. She sits down and watches him. After a moment, SONNY wakes up.

SONNY: Hello Mum.

LINA: I'm so angry with you.

SONNY: (*Weakly.*) You're meant to ask me how I'm feeling.

LINA: Why did you chuck your inhaler away?

SONNY: I didn't need it anymore…

LINA: That's clearly not true Sonny.

SONNY looks away.

I don't understand how you could have been so stupid.

SONNY: They test them on animals.

LINA: I don't care.

SONNY: I don't want animals to suffer and die because of me.

LINA: 'You don't want'. What about what I want?

Beat.

SONNY: What you want?

LINA: Yes. Me. And not just me, what about your sister? We've already lost someone who we loved very much, I don't want to have to go through that again. I'm meant to be the one who dies next, you can suffer and grieve, not me!

SONNY: I didn't die Mum.

LINA: You weren't far off it. It was a very severe attack.

SONNY: It might not be because I stopped my medication.

42

LINA: What?

SONNY: The doctor came round after you'd gone home.

LINA: Oh great, you wait all night to see someone, soon as you go they come round!

SONNY: He wants to see you later, he thinks it might have been the cats.

LINA: What cats?

SONNY: On the Cat Rescue. They think I might be allergic. That might be what triggered the attack.

Beat.

LINA: Really?

SONNY: They're going to do some tests.

LINA: Well, then, that's good isn't it? That means you'll just have to avoid cats and you'll be alright!

SONNY: (*Evasive.*) Maybe.

LINA: (*Knows something's wrong.*) What?

SONNY: They, er, said I might have to carry adrenaline round with me. So I can be injected with it if I have a sudden attack. But it will have been tested on animals.

LINA: Sonny.

SONNY: I don't want to take it Mum.

LINA: You have to!

SONNY: My asthma was fine before I went on the Pussy Cat Van. If I just avoid cats I should be fine.

LINA: What if you're not though?

SONNY: I will be.

LINA: What if you go into someone's house and there's cat hairs on the cushions or something and you don't realise?

SONNY: I won't.

LINA: Sonny!

SONNY: Leave it Mum!!

Pause. LINA fumes. SONNY looks glum. He tries to change the subject.

So, how's Raz? Did he like us?

LINA: After an enormous row and a near-death?

SONNY: He can't say we're boring anyway!

LINA: I've…put things on hold with Raz.

SONNY: What? Why? I thought he was a really nice bloke.

Pause. LINA sighs. Looks troubled.

LINA: I can't…think about Raz with all this going on with you.

SONNY: Don't blame it on me!

LINA: I'm just…not…very good at all that.

SONNY: All what?

LINA: You know. Men.

SONNY: That's because you don't practise enough. Chucking Raz isn't going to help!

LINA: Do we still call it chucking when we're over 40?

SONNY: Call it what you like, you're chickening out.

Pause. LINA sits down, looks in bag. Gives it to SONNY.

LINA: I brought you some clothes and magazines and stuff.

SONNY: Thanks.

LINA: Anita's coming later.

SONNY: (*Stony-faced.*) Is she.

Pause.

LINA: You were really horrible to her about your Dad.

SONNY shrugs, says nothing.

He loved you very much you know Sonny.

SONNY: (*Short.*) Did he.

LINA: He never…

SONNY: Cos apparently I 'don't remember'!

LINA: Anita didn't mean…

SONNY: (*Cutting in.*) I don't want to talk about it Mum.

Pause. LINA sighs.

Did Kelsey call? I was meant to meet her today.

LINA: Yes! I told her what happened. She wants to come and visit you.

SONNY: (*Looks a bit pleased.*) Does she?

LINA: Yes. 'Good friends' do visit each other in hospital you know.

SONNY: (*Smiles coyly.*) I know.

Beat. SONNY starts shuffling in the bag.

LINA: I knew there was a reason not to like cats.

SONNY: *Apart* from the fact that they poo in our garden?

LINA: I really don't know what you see in them.

SONNY: They're smart, they're independent and they know they're superior to human beings.

LINA: They're definitely arrogant, that's for sure.

SONNY: What, and humans aren't?

LINA: (*Beat.*) Good point.

SONNY: If cats were in charge things would be much more chilled.

LINA: We'd all have to eat mice. You wouldn't like that.

SONNY: We'd have to catch them first.

LINA: Or cat food, imagine that.

SONNY: (*Yawning.*) I'd be a vegetarian cat.

LINA: There aren't any vegetarian cats.
You'd have to eat meat, that's what cats do.

SONNY: (*Yawning more.*) I'd start a new thing. Cat vegetarianism.

LINA: Go back to sleep, smarty pants.

SONNY: Alright Mum.

SONNY closes his eyes. LINA looks troubled. Strokes his brow. End of scene.

Scene 6: Garden centre

LINA is sorting bulbs, she's deep in thought. RAZ comes in.
LINA doesn't see him.

RAZ: Er. Hi.

LINA jumps.

LINA: Oh! Hi.

RAZ: Sorry. I made you jump.

LINA: Yes.

Pause.

RAZ: You busy?

LINA: Yes.

RAZ: I've been wondering how Sonny was. Did you get
   my message?

LINA: Yes. Thank you. I've been meaning to call you
   back, he's...he's a lot better than he was.

RAZ: Good. That must be a relief.

LINA: Yes. It was a very bad attack.

RAZ: I know.

Pause.

Could we...have a word Lina?

LINA: I'm...sorting bulbs.

RAZ: Right.

LINA: They all have to be done by four o'clock.

RAZ: (*Glances at watch.*) It's only 10.30.

LINA: There's a lot of them.

RAZ: Can I meet you after work then?

LINA: I'm going to see Sonny at the hospital.

RAZ: Then when can I see you?

Pause.

LINA: I've been very busy Raz. You know. With Sonny and everything. He's been a bit down in the dumps since the attack. He could've died.

RAZ: I was there Lina. I do know.

LINA: Sorry.

Awkward pause.

RAZ: He's a nice kid, I really liked him.

LINA: He liked you too.

RAZ: Maybe I could go and see him? Cheer him up?

LINA: I dunno Raz…

RAZ: I could…come to the hospital with you tonight if you like? We could go for a drink afterwards.

LINA starts rocking back and forwards on her heels.

LINA: Raz, I don't think…

RAZ: What?

LINA: I don't think I can…

Pause.

RAZ: What?

LINA: I think we should just…leave it for now.

Beat.

RAZ: Is that 'Leave it for a couple of weeks until I stop worrying about Sonny' or is it 'Leave it, full stop'?

LINA: The thing is, I don't think I'll ever stop worrying about Sonny. Or Anita. That's just it. I thought we could, I mean I could…you know, now that they're both over eighteen and I was just about to have the house to myself, I thought a new relationship would be a good thing, but now he'll have to stay home and convalesce. He'll have to start late at University. I don't know if I would ever…

RAZ: (*Impatient.*) You're wittering again.

LINA: Sorry.

RAZ: Even if Sonny is still at home it doesn't mean you can't have a boyfriend.

LINA: (*Sniggers.*) Boyfriend. It makes us sound like teenagers!

RAZ: (*Serious.*) You're acting like a teenager.

LINA: What?

RAZ: (*Cross.*) If you don't want to have a relationship with me just say so. Don't ignore my calls. Don't tell me all this…stuff. About your kids. Sod your kids. What about me and you?!

Silence. LINA is shocked.

LINA: There's no need to raise your voice!

RAZ: I didn't raise my voice.

LINA: You did.

RAZ: I didn't!

LINA: You did.

RAZ: (*Raising voice.*) I thought we liked each other!!

LINA: We do!

RAZ: So what's the problem?

LINA: I…don't know.

RAZ: No. You don't. You've been thinking about the kids for so long you've forgotten how to think about yourself!

He goes to exit.

Give me a call when you've sorted your head out Lina.

He goes.

LINA: Raz!

He's gone. LINA looks kind of shocked and impressed at the same time. End of scene.

Scene 7: Hospital

SONNY is reading a magazine. ANITA hovers in the doorway. She has a piece of paper in her hand, an email she's printed up to show SONNY. SONNY looks up and sees her, looks away.

ANITA: Not speaking to me little bro?

SONNY: (*Irritated.*) Don't be silly.

ANITA comes in and sits next to the bed. SONNY continues to read the mag.

ANITA: I've, er, got some information for you. About asthma medicines.

SONNY: (*Still reading.*) What d'you mean, information?

ANITA: A friend of mine, a scientist, he does exactly the kind of asthma testing you're worried about. I thought it might help you to know what really goes on. Then you can make a clear decision about your medication.

SONNY: I've already made a clear decision.

ANITA: (*Getting up.*) Right. I'll go then.

SONNY: (*Looking up.*) He'll make it sound like nothing.

ANITA: I'm just trying to help Sonny.

Beat.

SONNY: (*Begrudging.*) Go on then.

ANITA: Sure?

SONNY: Go on. Before I change my mind.

ANITA: Okay. (*Sits back down.*) The mice used are genetically modified okay? They're created specially for testing asthma medicines.

SONNY: That doesn't make it okay Anita. Scientists playing God again.

ANITA: It means that they're exactly right for the tests, they get the most accurate results.

SONNY: They just see them as tools, not living breathing animals. Are you saying they deliberately create asthma-suffering mice?

ANITA: Yes.

SONNY: Oh great.

ANITA: (*Sighs.*) Am I going to get through this email or are you going to have a nervous breakdown on every single point?

SONNY: Go on.

ANITA: Okay. (*Reading.*) 'For asthma research we use the mouse's inhalation routes, which can be the whole body, or the nose only. Whole body is done in a special chamber. Nose only requires the animals to be restrained with plastic tubes.'

SONNY: So. They basically force them to inhale asthma drugs to see if it harms them?

ANITA: To see what the effects are, not just if it harms them. And force isn't the right word.

SONNY: Excuse me, 'restrained with plastic tubes'? They tie them down, they make them asthmatic so they can't breathe, so they feel just like I did, like I had a slab of concrete on my chest, choking me to death. Then they make them inhale something that may not even make them better!

ANITA: (*Shrugs.*) I don't think it's that bad.

SONNY: Not that bad! How would you like it? Why can't they find *another* way to test stuff?

ANITA: There isn't another way. Maybe in the future… [something will be developed]

SONNY: Not in my future.

ANITA: You might not have a future if you don't take the medication!

SONNY: How can I take it after what you've just told me?

ANITA: Look, Sonny, you just have to face it! You have no alternative. Yes, animals have suffered and died…

SONNY: (*Cutting in.*) They're still suffering and dying!

ANITA: Yes. But as little as possible and thousands of human lives are saved!! 1400 people in Britain still die from asthma every year. Imagine how big that would be if the work with animals hadn't been done.

SONNY: How many animals have died? I bet it's a lot more than 1400.

ANITA: I don't know! I don't care!

SONNY: You really don't care that animals are hurt, and sometimes hurt really badly?

ANITA: I care a bit but I care more about the people who benefit from it!

SONNY: That's like me saying it's alright for me to steal someone's money because I benefit from it.

ANITA: It's not!

SONNY: It is Anita! There must be other ways.

ANITA: Oh I give up!

She gets up.

You are so selfish.

SONNY: I'm selfish. What are you? You don't even think about animals, you're too busy thinking about your precious work.

ANITA: Will you change the record!!

SONNY: You change the record. You haven't even tried to see it from my point of view.

ANITA: What?

SONNY: You just assume that because you're cleverer than me, because you've taken loads of exams and read millions of books, then you're right. Mice are warm, living, breathing animals. What right have you got to hurt them?

ANITA: Alright...don't take your medication then. Don't bloody take it. Risk your life! Be a martyr for your... stupid cause. I wanted to help you but you've never accepted help from me. You just throw it back in my face every time. I don't know what I've done to make you hate me so much!!

ANITA leaves. She is near to tears.

SONNY: (*Amazed.*) Anita!

As ANITA goes out, RAZ comes in. They bump into each other.

ANITA: Mind where you're going!

RAZ: Sorry!

ANITA leaves, in a hurry.

(*To SONNY.*) Is she alright?

SONNY: Did she look like she was crying to you?

RAZ: Yeah, think so.

SONNY: (*Amazed/pleased.*) I've never made her cry before!

RAZ hovers. Pause.

I didn't expect to see you here.

RAZ: I hope you don't mind?

SONNY: Not at all. (*Ironic.*) Come and join the fun!

RAZ: I just wanted to...make sure you were okay. It was a real shock, seeing you like that. I didn't realise asthma could be that bad.

SONNY: You and me both.

Pause. Awkward silence.

RAZ: (*Re ANITA.*) What was that all about with your sister?

SONNY: Guess.

RAZ: 'The animal thing'?

SONNY: She won't even listen to me. She's always thought she knew everything. No wonder she became a scientist.

RAZ: She looked pretty upset for someone who knows everything.

SONNY: Only because I didn't back down. I really feel strongly about this Raz. She's never taken me seriously.

RAZ: That's big sisters for you.

RAZ sits down.

If it's any consolation, I agree with you.

SONNY: (*A bit taken aback.*) Do you?

RAZ: Yeah. In theory. It does seem wrong. It's a bit hard to do anything about it in practice though.

SONNY: No it's not! We can protest, we can refuse to join in, we can stop taking the medicines that are developed.

RAZ: Maybe. But not everyone feels angry enough to do that.

SONNY: They would if they knew.

RAZ: And I don't think it's just that that makes you angry with Anita.

Beat. SONNY looks away.

RAZ: All that stuff you said about your Dad. What was that all about?

SONNY: It's none of your business Raz.

RAZ: (*Beat.*) I suppose not.

Pause.

SONNY: Does Mum know you're here?

RAZ: I, er, said I might come.

SONNY: Yeah?

RAZ: (*Beat.*) Actually, she's given me the elbow.

SONNY: Oh. (*Embarrassed.*) That's a shame.

RAZ: Yeah. I was getting quite fond of your Mum.

SONNY: (*Amazed.*) Really?

RAZ: She was good fun.

SONNY: (*Astonished.*) Fun?

RAZ: Yes. Fun. And interesting. And clever. And kind. Am I embarrassing you?

SONNY: Slightly.

RAZ: (*Laughs.*) Sorry.

Pause.

SONNY: I knew she'd blame it on me.

RAZ: What?

SONNY: Breaking up with you.

RAZ: You don't think that's what it is then?

SONNY: No. I don't.

RAZ: What do you think it is?

SONNY: It's obvious. She's scared.

RAZ: Sacred of me?!

SONNY: (*Small laugh.*) Yeah. Mad isn't it?

RAZ: I'm a bit scared myself tell the truth. Starting a relationship with someone, it's a big change.

SONNY: I suppose so.

RAZ: Buddhists say change is inevitable.

SONNY: Do they?

RAZ: Yeah. Everything in the Universe. A constant process of change. If you can accept that, and realise you can't control it, then life is maybe more easy to deal with.

SONNY: What if you don't want to accept it?

RAZ: You're very like your Mum you know Sonny.

SONNY: Am I?

RAZ: Yeah. You both have a very fixed view of things. What if you thought about this animal testing thing in a different way?

SONNY: What way?

RAZ: What if you thought to yourself, 'I am going to take the medication'?

SONNY: I can't!

RAZ: I'm not saying you should do it. Just think about it. I mean, you could say, if I don't take the medication and I get ill, that's one less person protesting. One less person doing something. Then what will all the animals who've been killed developing your asthma drugs have died for?

Beat. SONNY thinks.

SONNY: What's the Buddhists' view about animal rights?

RAZ: Ah. They say that no living thing should be harmed, if you can help it. We all breathe the same air don't we? Animals and humans. Every breath is precious. Breathing's very important to Buddhists.

SONNY: It's very important to me!

Pause. SONNY reflects.

Do Buddhists believe in God?

RAZ: That's a big question.

SONNY: (*Quietly. Frightened.*) I nearly died Raz. I've been... I was really scared.

RAZ: I don't blame you mate.

SONNY: What if there's...nothing? What if I stick to my guns over this and I die and there's nothing? I'm only eighteen.

RAZ: On the other hand, maybe there's something.

SONNY: (*Hopeful.*) Do you believe in a God?

RAZ: Haven't got a clue mate. They haven't proved it either way have they?

SONNY: (*Disappointed.*) I guess not.

RAZ: A lot of Buddhists believe in reincarnation.

SONNY: Yeah. I don't know if I like that. What if I came back as a laboratory animal?

RAZ: What if you came back as a scientist who experiments on laboratory animals?

SONNY: I don't know which one would be worse!

RAZ: Buddhists believe everything in life is interconnected. No-one is entirely separate from anyone or anything else. If that's true, then we should all be looking after each other. Animals, humans.

SONNY: Scientists.

RAZ: Sisters.

SONNY: Brothers.

RAZ: Bus drivers.

SONNY: Train drivers.

RAZ: Pigs.

SONNY: Pandas.

RAZ: Pelicans.

SONNY: Policemen.

RAZ: Traffic wardens.

SONNY: Vultures.

RAZ: Tarantulas.

SONNY: Cockroaches.

RAZ: Dinner ladies.

SONNY: Teachers.

RAZ: Turtles.

SONNY: Tortoises.

RAZ: Tabby cats.

SONNY: Tom cats.

RAZ: She cats.

SONNY: Mothers.

RAZ: Mothers' boyfriends.

SONNY sniggers.

SONNY: Bit old to be called a boyfriend Raz.

RAZ: Partner then.

More sniggering.

That's what she does.

SONNY: What?

RAZ: Sniggers anytime I say anything personal.

SONNY: Sorry!

End of scene.

Scene 8: Garden centre

ANITA is standing next to a container which is about to be potted up. Her eyes are red from crying. After a bit LINA comes in carrying a plant to put in the pot. She sees ANITA.

LINA: Hello darling!

ANITA: Hi.

LINA: Are you alright? (*Amazed.*) You look like you've been cry…

ANITA: I'm fine.

LINA: You sure?

ANITA: (*Lying.*) I think I might have a bit of a cold coming on that's all.

LINA: How did it go at the hospital?

ANITA: Very badly.

LINA: Is he still…?

ANITA: (*Angry.*) Still as stubborn as ever, stupid little…kid.

LINA: (*Sighs.*) Well. I suppose if he doesn't want to do it we can't make him.

ANITA: Sometimes I think he's just doing all this to have a go at me.

LINA: Oh no. No Anita, he really does care about animals, he's always been like that hasn't he? Maybe if I'd let him have a pet when he was little he would've got it out of his system.

ANITA: But he seems to think I'm some kind of monster.

LINA: He doesn't darling.

ANITA: I have done a course, you know, to get my licence to perform experiments on animals.

LINA: Oh yes?

ANITA: And we really do have to make sure that the animals suffer as little as possible.

LINA: Good.

Beat. ANITA looks a bit uneasy.

ANITA: If I tell you something will you promise not to tell Sonny?

LINA: Cross my heart.

ANITA: It did make me think a bit. Doing that course.

LINA: Did it?

ANITA: When you think about it, why should we have the right, it is quite a hard question to answer.

LINA: Well, I suppose because we're superior, we've got bigger brains and more strength. So we can.

ANITA: I don't know about superior. We haven't exactly made the world a brilliant place have we?

LINA: Some of it's brilliant.

ANITA: In fact, we've pretty much messed up the whole planet.

LINA: Not all of it. Not all of us.

ANITA: And Sonny's right you know, about Dad. All the research that's been done on leukaemia, all the animals that have suffered, they still didn't cure him did they?

Pause. LINA takes ANITA's hand.

LINA: It's not your fault your dad died. It's not your fault Sonny's ill.

ANITA: I went into science for Dad, so he'd be proud of me. Remember what he used to say? It's not politics that changes the world Anita, it's inventions. It's progress. It's science.

LINA: Come here.

LINA gives ANITA a hug. ANITA struggles with tears for a moment then cries.

You're just like him. Just like your Dad.

They hug for a moment. ANITA breaks free, wipes her tears away, recovers herself.

ANITA: I'm sorry if I…

LINA: What?

ANITA: I know I'm sometimes a bit…sarcastic. And not very friendly. I don't mean to be. It's just… I get nervous.

LINA: I know darling.

ANITA: I hope I haven't put Raz off.

LINA: Oh. Raz.

ANITA: Because you really like him.

LINA: Do I?

ANITA: Yes. You squeezed his hand, when he made a joke at dinner and no-one laughed.

LINA: *(Bashful.)* I never!

ANITA: Yes you did Mum. I haven't seen you do that since Dad.

Pause. LINA is taken aback.

It's alright, you know. To move on. To be with someone else. You've been on your own for a long time now.

LINA: I haven't been on my own. I've been with you. And Sonny.

ANITA: That's not what I mean.

Pause. LINA rocks.

Please apologise to Raz for me. When you see him. I was a bit…short with him at the hospital.

LINA: What? Was he at the hospital?

ANITA: Yeah.

LINA: Really?

ANITA: Yeah. Didn't he tell you he was going?

LINA: Not ex…actly.

ANITA: Have you and him fallen out or something?

LINA: Not ex…actly.

ANITA: Mum. If you really like him please don't…

LINA: What?

ANITA: Mess it up.

LINA: Who says I have?

ANITA: If you're with Raz I can stop worrying.

LINA: Worrying?

ANITA: Yes. About you.

LINA: You don't need to worry about me darling.

ANITA: Yes I do!

LINA: But… I'm the one who does the worrying!

ANITA: I hear you you know. In the middle of the night. Crying and that.

LINA: Oh Anita. Everyone cries in the wee small hours sometimes.

ANITA: I used to get those nightmares, d'you remember? About Dad coming back to life again. I'd be so happy. And then I'd realise there was something funny about him. Something not quite right.

LINA: I remember.

ANITA: It was someone else. An impostor. Pretending to be my Dad. A dead person with dead eyes. And he wanted to kill you, d'you remember? He wanted to take you back with him to his grave.

LINA: (*Goes to hug ANITA.*) Darling.

ANITA: (*Shrugs her off.*) And then I'd wake up and you'd be crying, and I'd hear you, and I was so worried, and I still am worried, because you're still crying, even when I went off to University, and I'd really like you to stop crying now because I'd really like to stop worrying!

Pause. LINA takes ANITA's hand. Silence. LINA is very moved.

LINA: I'll try and sort things out with Raz, okay?

ANITA: Good.

LINA: You really are a very lovely girl you know.

ANITA: You've never called me that before. Lovely. You usually say clever.

LINA: Do I darling?

ANITA: Mum?

LINA: Yeah?

ANITA: You won't tell Sonny will you?

LINA: Tell him what?

ANITA: That I was, em, upset.

LINA: Course I won't sweetheart.

LINA hugs ANITA. ANITA lets her. End of scene.

Scene 9: Garden centre, a few days later. Shelving area

RAZ comes on in overalls and starts hammering nails into the shelves. After a moment, LINA comes on. RAZ sees her and stops hammering. They both feel a bit awkward.

LINA: Hi.

RAZ: Hi.

Pause.

How are you?

LINA: I'm fine. You?

RAZ: Alright. How's Sonny?

LINA: He's feeling a lot better. He's coming out of hospital on Monday!

RAZ: Good. Glad to hear it.

Beat.

LINA: He, er, said you'd been to see him.

RAZ: Yes. I hope you don't mind.

LINA: He told me off!

RAZ: Oh yes?

LINA: Him and Anita, they both told me off.

RAZ: Oh yes? What for?

LINA: For, em, you know.

RAZ: No.

LINA: For, well, putting things on hold. With you.

RAZ: Ah. They've been on hold have they? I thought you'd chucked me.

LINA giggles.

LINA: No. I haven't chucked you. Have you chucked me?

RAZ: Mm. Let me think about that.

RAZ pretends to think.

LINA: If you have, you need to get a friend to tell me.

RAZ: Eh?

LINA: Like at school. You know (*Mimicking teenage boy.*) 'Raz's chucked you. Sorry'. You did say I was behaving like a teenager.

RAZ: Alright, in that case my mate's got another message. 'Raz says, will you go back out with him?'

LINA: (*Smiling.*) Tell Raz I'll think about it.

RAZ: Tell her not to think about it too long. Raz's got a queue of women desperate to go out with him.

LINA: Is that true?

RAZ: Nah. Sounds good though. Keeps the women interested.

LINA: I'm interested anyway.

RAZ: Are you?

LINA: Yeah.

Pause.

RAZ: Will we be going steady now then?

LINA: Not yet. After three months, that's going steady.

RAZ: So we're still just dating?

LINA: Yes. But it's looking quite promising.

RAZ: That'll do for me.

Pause. They both smile big smiles at each other.

LINA: I'd, er, better get going. I'm cutting back the climbing plants today, it's taking me ages!

RAZ: Okay. What time's your lunch?

LINA: 12.30.

RAZ: Meet me behind the bike sheds?

LINA: We haven't got any bike sheds.

RAZ: Garden furniture?

LINA: Alright then.

LINA exits, smiling. RAZ watches her go.

RAZ: (*After she's gone.*) Yes!

End of scene.

Scene 10: LINA's kitchen, the following Monday

ANITA is next to the table, which has a bottle of fizzy wine and four glasses on it. There is a banner on the wall, it reads 'Welcome Home Sonny'. ANITA looks nervous. After a moment the door goes. We hear voices off then in comes SONNY, with his mum fussing over him. RAZ follows, carrying SONNY's holdall. RAZ is wearing a T-shirt with 'What would Scooby do?' written on it.

SONNY: Mum, you're practically carrying me! I'm alright!

LINA: Okay Bossy Boots.

LINA leaves SONNY alone. SONNY sees ANITA.

SONNY: (*Cross.*) Oh. I didn't think you were going to be here.

ANITA: Well I am.

A moment's silence.

LINA: Sorry it took so long. Raz' car's a bit of an old banger!

RAZ: Ay!

LINA: Sorry! It was very kind of you to offer a lift.

Beat. SONNY's still not happy to see ANITA. ANITA looks embarrassed.

RAZ: Shall we crack open the fizz then?

LINA: Yes please Raz. Sonny, please sit down.

RAZ opens the wine and pours. SONNY, ANITA and LINA sit down at the table.

Welcome home darling! Cheers!

They all clink glasses. SONNY avoids ANITA's glass.

ANITA: Oh for crying out…

LINA: Anita.

ANITA: He won't clink glasses with me!

LINA: We've only just got home. Let's…try not to have an argument for at least five minutes!

ANITA: I don't want an argument.

SONNY: I do.

LINA: Sonny!

SONNY: I've got something to tell you. About the asthma testing.

LINA: Oh not again!

RAZ: (*Holding his hand out.*) Lina.

LINA: What.

RAZ: Let's leave them to it shall we?

LINA: But…

RAZ: Let them sort it out themselves eh?

LINA: (*Doubtful.*) If you really think… [so]

RAZ grabs LINA's hand and yanks her offstage. Pause.

ANITA: (*American.*) 'Bring it on little bro.'

SONNY: Don't call me that. You told me there were no alternatives.

ANITA: I did.

SONNY: I told my friend Kelsey and she did some research for me at Animal Kind.

ANITA: And?

SONNY: Testing drugs on animals doesn't even always work!

ANITA: What? Doesn't work? What d'you mean?

SONNY: Some drugs actually harmed and killed humans, despite the fact that they were safety tested on animals.

ANITA: (*Very doubtful.*) That's pretty rare Sonny.

SONNY: Using animals at all may have hindered research. All this time, they've been going up blind alleys because animals aren't similar enough to us.

ANITA: Sonny, animals are much more similar to humans than you think. Mice are genetically over 90% the same as us.

SONNY: So then why are they trying to develop other ways of testing and researching diseases?

ANITA: What other ways?

SONNY: Lung tissue from human volunteers is being used for asthma research, amongst other things.

ANITA: Okay. And your point is?

SONNY: You said I had no alternative. But alternatives are being researched right now. They just need to put more money into it.

ANITA: I agree.

SONNY: (*Beat.*) You agree?

ANITA: I'd rather they used other methods too. I just don't think there are enough viable alternatives right now.

SONNY: You said there was no other way. But scientists can use scanning machines, computers, clinical studies, human tissues.

ANITA: (*Sighs.*) Those are things that are still developing. It doesn't mean they're ready to take over from animals. And in my kind of research, I'm researching the animal itself. A computer can't take its place.

SONNY: Then don't do that kind of research.

Pause. ANITA looks sad.

ANITA: I don't think you and I are ever going to agree about this.

SONNY: You won't listen to me.

ANITA: I do listen. I wish I agreed with you.

SONNY: No you don't.

ANITA: You're my brother Sonny. I don't want you to hate me.

SONNY: I don't hate you. Why d'you keep saying that?

ANITA: I feel like you do.

SONNY: I don't!

ANITA: Can't we just…drop this?

SONNY: Not if you're going to be walking into that lab every day and I'm leafleting outside!

Pause. ANITA sighs.

ANITA: Dad really loved animals you know.

SONNY: Did he?

ANITA: Yeah. He wanted us to have a dog! A big family dog, but Mum wouldn't let him.

SONNY: I didn't know that. Typical Mum!

ANITA: I'm not sure about pets though. It's really just another way we take advantage of animals isn't it? For our own comfort, not for theirs.

SONNY: Well yeah. But I'd rather us taking advantage than someone else neglecting them!

ANITA: (*Thinks.*) Good point.

SONNY: (*Taken aback.*) Good point?

ANITA: Yeah.

SONNY: Blimey. You've never said that to me before.

ANITA: It's the first good point you've ever made.

SONNY pulls tongues at her. She smiles.

SONNY: (*Beat.*) Would've been nice. Me and Dad in the park with…Bonzo!

ANITA: Bonzo! What a crap name. I would've called him Elvis. Or Kevin, something like that.

SONNY: No way! Elvis. You're just trying to be trendy.

Beat.

(*Quickly.*) He never said goodbye to me you know.

ANITA: Who never?

SONNY: Dad.

ANITA: (*Confused.*) Never said goodbye?

SONNY: No. Don't you remember? It was just you and Mum in the room when he…died. No one asked me to come in.

ANITA: I don't remember that.

SONNY: I just sat in my bedroom and when it was over no one said a thing to me. I didn't even know until they came and took his body away. I saw them, carrying his body out, and no one had told me.

ANITA: Oh Sonny.

She goes to hug him. He moves away.

SONNY: I thought he might have asked for me.

ANITA: Sonny, he was too far gone to ask for anything.

SONNY: Then why didn't you or Mum ask me in?

ANITA: I was eleven. I was devastated Sonny. I didn't even notice. I guess Mum was the same. I'm so sorry.

Pause. They both don't know what to say.

SONNY: (*Hard to say.*) I've decided to take my asthma medicine, by the way. If I need it.

ANITA: (*Big relief.*) Oh thank God.

SONNY: I still don't agree with it. But I can't go on campaigning against your lab if I'm in hospital all the time can I?

ANITA: I'd rather have you leafleting outside the lab than in hospital any day. What about the adrenaline?

SONNY: Don't need it. I'm not allergic to cats after all. Didn't Mum tell you?

ANITA: No.

SONNY: Another thing that slipped her mind.

ANITA: Don't be hard on Mum Sonny. She dotes on you.

Pause. SONNY looks away.

She'll be feeling awful guilty you know, after your attack. She'll want to make it up to you.

SONNY: What d'you mean?

ANITA: Just that, well, now we know you're not allergic to cats…

SONNY: (*Twigging.*) Ye-es.

ANITA: A fluffy wuffy pussy cat would be just the thing to cheer you up.

Beat. SONNY twigs.

SONNY: You really are very clever aren't you.

ANITA shrugs.

ANITA: I don't like to go on about it.

SONNY: Raz likes animals too! We could get him on our side.

ANITA: Good thinking.

SONNY: It has to be a rescue cat, I'm not having one of those special breeds.

ANITA: Fine by me. Shall we go and ask her? While the guilt's still fresh?

SONNY: After you.

ANITA: Thank you.

SONNY lets ANITA go past. As she goes past he kind of half trips her up. Something he used to do when they were kids. ANITA stumbles.

(*Cross.*) Sonny!

SONNY: Got you!

ANITA stops being cross, gets a gleam in her eye.

ANITA: Right. You're dead little bro.

She goes to grab him, he dodges out of the way.

SONNY: You'll have to catch me first.

ANITA: Oh will I?!

He runs offstage. ANITA runs after him, laughing.

End of play.

THE USE OF ANIMALS IN MEDICAL RESEARCH

Every Breath Teachers' Resource

Contents

The aim of these triggers is to deepen the students' understanding of the issues posed by the use of animals in medical research. This is done through the provision of a range of key discussion triggers stimulated by the characters and the dilemmas that confront them.

- Trigger 1: Is it different to test on monkeys and dogs than it is on rats?
- Trigger 2: What responsibilities do we have to animals?
- Trigger 3: What rights to protest should people have? What about the right to carry out legal research?
- Trigger 4: How can the public find out what takes place inside laboratories that conduct experiments?
- Trigger 5: Some research is aimed at gaining knowledge about how the body works, and may result in helping us better understand illness. Is it still okay to use animals in these experiments?
- Trigger 6: Research into life-threatening illness involves some suffering, or the death of thousands of animals. Is that okay?
- Trigger 7: What does the Buddhist perspective teach us?
- Trigger 8: Is it right to use genetically modified animals in research?

Introduction

Every Breath explores the serious social, moral, scientific and political questions raised by the use of animals in medical research, and is the sixth in the Creating the Debate series of projects developed and produced by Y Touring. A Society Award from the Wellcome Trust and a contribution from the Association of Medical Research Charities funded this project.

Aims

Every Breath aims, through theatre and debate, to:

- Inform target audiences of the range of scientific, social, moral and political views surrounding this issue
- Encourage and stimulate informed debate
- Provide an impartial forum for learning through debate

Included in these resources are:

- The Consensus Statement from the report, *The Ethics of Research Involving Animals*, by the Nuffield Council on Bioethics
- The synopsis of the play by playwright Judith Johnson
- An outline of the characters and how they relate to the issues raised in the play
- Suggested Preparatory Lessons
- A Glossary

Preparatory Lessons

If short on time, we suggest that you prioritise the 'What does it mean' and the 'What do we think' activities, as they offer the most direct way to set-up both the play and the debate.

Consensus Statement

Taken from *The Ethics of Research Involving Animals*
A report produced by The Nuffield Council on Bioethics

Research involving animals and other uses of animals

It is important to consider the ethical issues raised by animal experimentation in the wider context of the other uses of animals in society, and to take into account:

- The impact on the lives and welfare of animals that different uses have
- The broader consequences if there were a ban on using animals in specific circumstances
- A comparison of the benefits arising from the different uses of animals
- The numbers of animals involved

The involvement of animals in research cannot be justified simply by the fact that animals are used or abused in other ways. Each use requires special consideration. Members of the Working Party noted during their own discussions and in considering responses to the Consultation that views on animal research were not always consistent with views on other uses of animals. Awareness that contradictory views are often held simultaneously is an important first step in considering the ethical issues raised by animal research.

The benefits of research involving animals

Historically, animals have been used in a wide range of scientific research activities that have provided many benefits to society, particularly in relation to the advancement of scientific knowledge, human and veterinary medicine, and the safety of chemical products.

Some of these advances might have been achieved by other means, although we cannot know this. Neither can we know what a world would look like in which animal research had never been undertaken. Hypothetically, there may have been other options which could have produced acceptable levels of knowledge and healthcare. These levels might have been lower than our current standards, but perhaps if society had deemed the use of animals for research as unacceptable, there would have been acceptance of greater limitations on scientific and medical progress. Alternatively, it is conceivable that equally good or better progress might have been achieved with other methods. The Working Party agrees that speculation about whether or not acceptable standards in basic and applied research could have been achieved in the past by means other than the use of animals is less important than the question of assessing the consequences of continuing or abandoning animal experimentation now.

It is sometimes assumed that to end animal research would be to end scientific and medical progress, but such generalisation is unhelpful. The UK Government has responded to changes in the moral climate by introducing policies that have ended some types of animal research and testing in the UK. For example, the use of animals for the testing of cosmetic products and their ingredients, alcohol and tobacco has ceased. Similar policies are in place regarding the use of the great apes. Independent of the moral acceptability of research, the scientific costs and benefits of abandoning specific types of animal research need to be assessed on a case-by-case basis. On the one hand, the possibility of the emergence of new diseases may require a reassessment of whether the abandonment of specific types of research is still justified. On the other, scientific advances that could replace the use of animals in some areas may enjoin us to assess whether further policies should be introduced to terminate these uses of animals accordingly.

The validity, usefulness and relevance of specific types of animal research, for example in relation to the use of animals for the study of human diseases, needs to be ascertained in each individual case.

Desirability of a world without animal research

All research licensed in the UK under the Animal (Scientific Procedures) Act 1986 (A(SP)A) has the potential to cause pain, suffering, distress or lasting harm to the animals used. Most animals are killed at the end of experiments. A world in which the important benefits of such research could be achieved without causing pain, suffering, distress, lasting harm or death to animals involved in research must be the ultimate goal.

We have considered the different arguments advanced in favour and against continuing specific types of animal research in Chapters 3 and 14. Some believe the imperative to protect animal welfare should be overriding, whereas others believe that the moral arguments favour the continuation of research on animals. All members of the Working Party acknowledged that these viewpoints arise from moral convictions that should be given serious consideration. This approach requires open-mindedness in trying to understand the reasons and arguments of others. Genuine willingness is also required to test and, where necessary, revise one's own moral framework.

While we trust that more progress in the moral debate can be made, we are aware that, for the near future, further moral argument alone cannot provide a universal answer as to whether or not research on animals is justified. But practical advances in scientific methods can reduce areas of conflict. For this reason, the importance of the 'Three Rs' (Refinement, Reduction and Replacement), and especially of the need to find Replacements, cannot be overstated.

The ethical importance of the Three Rs

The Working Party therefore concludes that it is crucial that the Three Rs are, and continue to be, enshrined in UK regulation on research involving animals. The principle that animals may only be used for research if there is no other way of obtaining the results anticipated from an experiment is also fundamental. Furthermore, we observe that for moral justification of animal research it is insufficient to consider only those alternatives, which are practicably available at the time of assessing a licence application. The question of why alternatives are not available and what is required to make them available must also be asked. The potential of the Three Rs is far from being exhausted. The Working Party therefore agrees that there is a moral imperative to develop as a priority scientifically rigorous and validated alternative methods for those areas in which Replacements do not currently exist. It is equally important to devise mechanisms that help in the practical implementation of available validated methods.

In applying the Three Rs it is crucial to consider not only the context of the experiments themselves but also the many other factors that can affect animal welfare, including breeding, transportation, feeding, housing, and handling. The quality of these factors and especially the ability of animals to satisfy their species-specific needs can usually be improved.

Regulation

We acknowledge that the UK has the most detailed legislative framework concerning research on animals in the world. But proper attention to the welfare of animals involved in research and the accountability of scientists who conduct research on animals cannot be achieved merely by having detailed regulations. Regulation can act as an emotional screen between the researcher and an animal, possibly encouraging researchers to believe that simply to conform to regulations is to act in a moral way. It is therefore crucial to promote best practice more actively and to improve the culture of care in establishments licensed to conduct experiments on animals.

When considering the replacement of specific types of research by alternative methods, it is important to take account of the international context in which research involving animals takes place. Many chemical and pharmaceutical compounds that have been developed are being marketed in countries or regions that have different regulatory frameworks for animal research and testing. There is a range of alternatives that have been internationally accepted for safety testing. Nonetheless, many Replacements are not universally accepted, and the process of validation is lengthy.

These processes need to be optimised and initiatives aimed at abandoning and replacing specific types of animal testing at national levels complemented by initiatives at the international level. This is not to say that initiatives in the UK can only be taken once there is consensus at an international level. In the past, the UK has been a leader in working towards change in international policies related to research involving animals. This leadership should be encouraged.

Duplication of experiments on animals

Scientific experiments involving animals are sometimes repeated by the same or other research groups. In considering whether the repetition of such experiments should take place, it is important to distinguish between *duplication* and *replication* of experiments:*

- Duplication of harmful animal experiments is in principle unacceptable. We use the term to describe cases where there is insufficient scientific justification for the repetition. It occurs primarily when the scientist either does not know that another has carried out the experiment or test in question, or when he does know, but is unable to attain reasonable access to the information.

- Replication refers to repetition of experiments or tests where this is necessary for sound progress in scientific enquiries. The scientific method demands that research findings need to be corroborated by the same and other research groups, in order to establish the validity of the results.

The Working Party acknowledges that academic competitiveness and commercial confidentiality can sometimes complicate the sharing of information. But at its best, science is an open process, and mechanisms that prevent the sharing of information need to be reviewed carefully in terms of their justification and implications for the use of animals in research.

The context of the debate

The majority of researchers who use animals consider that despite progress in the implementation of the Three Rs, animal research will remain an essential part of their work. Furthermore, certain provisions in the current regulatory framework for approval of chemical products and medicines require tests involving animals. We conclude that it is unrealistic to assume that all animal experimentation will end in the short term. It is crucial, therefore, to create a climate in which the necessity and justification for using animals is assessed and discussed fairly and with due respect for all views.

Constructive debate would be facilitated by the provision of clear information about the full implications of research involving animals in terms of the kind, numbers and species of animals used, as well as the pain, suffering and distress to which they can be subjected. It is equally important that society should be informed about the scientific, medical and other benefits of research involving animals. Information about selected aspects of research without provision of any further context can be misleading.

All members of the Working Party agree that the use of violence and intimidation against members of the research community, research institutions, their business partners, family and neighbours, or against organisations and people representing animal welfare groups, is morally wrong and politically insidious. The freedom to promote or oppose research involving animals peacefully and democratically, however, must be maintained.

---

*   Sometimes, animals are used in repeated experiments for the purpose of education or training. However, we have not addressed the issues raised by this particular use here.

The Play: The Synopsis

18 year-old Sonny believes strongly that medical research involving animals is wrong. He is an active, gentle young man, much loved by everyone who knows him. Anita, 21, his sister, is a scientist. She is confident, vivacious and smart. She is also completely convinced that research involving animals is justified. Their mother Lina doesn't know what to think; to her children's continued annoyance she can see both sides of the argument. Frankly, she's much more interested in how her relationship with Raz is going to play out, especially when he meets her kids.

Raz is a quirky kind-hearted ageing ex-punk. He is a breath of fresh air for Lina, who has struggled on her own for years to bring up her two kids, and who has a tendency to take life too seriously. Raz has recently discovered Buddhism.

Although not fully converted, he is interested in the teachings of Buddha and is able to take a spiritual view on animal testing. Which is that all life is connected, human and animal, and we should try not to kill or harm other living beings.

An early scene in the play takes place at a family meal where Raz is introduced. Although things go quite well at first, the meal breaks down when Sonny and Anita have a blazing row about animal research. Sonny cannot see why scientists persist in using animal experimentation when, as far as he's concerned, the experiments don't help, and can in fact hinder medical progress. Lina despairs. The meal is totally disrupted however, when Sonny has an enormous asthma attack. He has not been taking his asthma medication because it is tested on animals. He's rushed to hospital.

In hospital, Sonny undergoes tests to find out what triggered his attack. The doctors think it is the cats he has recently been handling as a volunteer at the local cat rescue centre. The attack leaves Sonny feeling depressed. He still doesn't want to take his medication and his Mum and Anita are very angry with him. Lina is in a martyred panic. She finishes her relationship with Raz. She feels that starting a relationship when Sonny is ill is wrong. Anita is horrified. Sonny is stupid and he gets on her nerves, but she doesn't want him to get ill and die! She tries to explain to him exactly what happens when asthma products are researched and tested on animals, but Sonny won't listen.

Lina pleads with Sonny but it is no use. Sonny sees in the suffering of animals a parallel with his own suffering. He won't budge.

Raz, never one to give up easily, will not let Lina end their relationship.

He has built up quite a good connection with Sonny and insists on seeing him. Maybe, despite Raz's own beliefs, he can persuade Sonny to take his medication? They talk about spirituality, about what death means, what suffering means, to both animals and humans. Sonny is calmed and reassured.

When Sonny comes out of hospital, he challenges Anita about some of her views. She has said there is no alternative to animal testing, but Sonny finds out that alternatives are being researched and developed. The doctors have found out he isn't allergic to cats. Sonny decides to go back to taking his asthma medication, but only so he can continue to protest about animal research and testing. Anita says that she may never agree with Sonny, but she'd rather see him leafleting outside her Lab than lying in a hospital bed. At the end of the play an uneasy truce is established between brother and sister. Lina, free from worry (for the time being!), is able to re-establish her relationship with Raz.

Judith Johnson
November 2005

Issues raised in the Play

Every Breath explores the complex ideological and emotional issues that surround the use of animals in medical research. It aims to get the audience to question any preconceptions they may have and to encourage serious debate of these issues.

- Is it different to test on monkeys and dogs than rats and fruit flies? If it is then why is it?
- What responsibilities do we as a race have to animals?
- Research into life-threatening illness involves some suffering, or the death of, thousands of animals. Is that okay?
- And what about research that is aimed at gaining knowledge about how the body works, and may as a result help us better understand illness? Is it still okay to use animals here?
- And most crucially, is human life more important than animal life? And if so, just how much more important is it?

Sonny – Aged 18, is a vegetarian and a non-violent animal rights activist who's just finished his A-levels. He is totally against the use of animals in medical research, but is forced to examine his principles carefully when his own life is threatened.

Anita – 21 years old and Sonny's sister, is a science graduate about to do a PhD. Anita's a carnivore who's always disagreed with her brother about the rights of animals. Her work leads her to realise that whilst there may not be an alternative to the use of animals that she considers viable, she really wishes there was.

Lina – Is 40…something, works at the local garden centre whilst trying (and generally failing) to keep the peace between the rival camps represented by her offspring. Lina's been a single parent since the death of her husband from leukaemia ten years ago.

Raz – Late thirties/early forties, is a painter and decorator. Trying to have a relationship with Sonny and Anita's mum Lina is not easy whilst the family is at war over the use or abuse, depending on who you ask, of animals. However, the fact that he is considering becoming Buddhist does give Raz an interesting perspective on the argument.

What does it mean ?

Objective

A brainstorming exercise to ensure that your students are familiar with the key terms and phrases referred to in the play.

Materials

Flipchart & Whiteboard.

Process

1 Explain that you are going to say a word or phrase and that when you call out their name, you want each of your students to say the first word that comes into their head.
2 Explain that if they can't think of a word or if their mind goes blank, they can say pass.
3 After each round clarify the actual meaning of the word or phrase if appropriate, and discuss as a class some of the associations that have been shared.

Words & Phrases

Medical Research   Animal Rights   Testing   Leukaemia

Protester   Viable Alternative   Treatments   Clinical Trials

Asthma   Buddhism   Vivisection

What do we feel?

Objective
To explore the emotions associated with some of the key phrases associated with the use of animals in medical research.

Materials
Flipchart & Whiteboard.

Process
1 Using the list of words below, repeat the above activity asking your students to think of an emotion rather than an adjective that they associate with the word or phrase.
2 After you have completed the activity, ask your students if they want to comment on the groups responses.

Words & Phrases

Scientists   Protesters   Doctors

Intimidation   Animal Research   Life Saving Treatments

Violence   Medical Progress   Exploitation

Sculpture

Objective
To enable a non-verbal student exploration of pre-conceptions about scientists and animal rights protesters.

Materials
Ideally a large space i.e. drama studio, a cleared classroom.

Process
Split the class into groups of three – A, B and C (the odd group of four is fine).

A's, you are the sculptor, B and C (+ D's if required) you are the sculptor's clay. I want the sculptor to guide the clay into a picture that I will describe.

After each one, invite the whole group to look at each other's sculptures and comment on what they see.

Sculpture One
Sculpt an image of a scientist who experiments on animals.

Sculpture Two
Sculpt an image of an animal rights activist who fights for animal rights.

What do we think?

Objective

To ascertain current understanding of the issues. The debate will explore what your students think about the use or misuses of the outcomes of brain research.

Materials

A large space e.g. drama studio, a cleared classroom.

Process

1 Ask your students to stand in the centre of the space.
2 Explain that there is an imaginary line running down the centre of the space, one end of the line represents Agree and the opposite end of the line represents Disagree. The middle of the line is Don't Know.
3 Explain that you are going to read out a series of statements. If they agree with the statement they should go and stand at the end of the line that is Agree. If they disagree they should go and stand at the end of the line that is Disagree. If they are not sure or don't know what they think they should stay in the middle.
4 After they have taken up their positions, ask your students to explain why they have chosen their position. After hearing from several students – give your group the opportunity of changing their position.
5 Repeat the process for each statement.

Statements

1 It is right to use animals to help find cures for diseases such as cancer that can lead to the death of human beings.
2 It is wrong to experiment on animals.
3 The life of an animal is as valuable as that of a human being.
4 It is right to use mice and rats in medical research but not cats, dogs or monkeys.
5 Animals should have the basic right not to be harmed or killed.
6 I understand why some animals rights activists might, because of their beliefs, use violence and intimidation against companies and individuals.
7 The law ensures that animals used in medical research are looked after properly.
8 Humans should be used for medical research instead of animals.
9 There should be more research into the alternatives to the use of animals in medical research.
10 The Government should ban all experiments on animals because animal-based research is unnecessary.
11 People should have the right to protest peacefully outside laboratories that use animals in medical research.
12 It would be wrong to stop using animals in medical research before viable non-animal alternatives are found.

Glossary

A) Asthma

A chronic respiratory disease, often arising from allergies, characterised by sudden recurring attacks of breathing difficulties, chest tightness, and coughing.

B) Animal Rights

The right to humane treatment claimed on behalf of animals, especially the right not to be exploited for human purposes. The animal rights movement includes a diverse range of individuals and groups concerned with protecting animals from perceived abuse or misuse. Supporters are specifically concerned with the use of animals for medical research, cosmetic testing (now banned in the UK), the killing of animals for furs, hunting for pleasure, and the raising of livestock in restrictive or inhumane conditions, known by some as factory farming. Some also wish to outlaw the keeping of all pets. Concern for inhumane treatment of animals has led many supporters of the movement to advocate vegetarianism. Although the movement can trace its roots to the anti-vivisection campaigns (see **Vivisection**) of the nineteenth century, the modern movement is closely tied to environmental issues.

C) Buddhism

The religion represented by the many groups, particularly numerous in Asia, that follow the teachings of Buddha. In brief, these are that life is permeated with suffering caused by desire, that suffering ceases when desire ceases, and that enlightenment obtained through right conduct, wisdom, and meditation releases one from desire and therefore suffering, and rebirth.

D) Leukaemia

Leukaemia is a type of cancer, which affects the blood and can be fatal. Cancer is a group of more than 100 diseases that have two important things in common. One is that certain cells in the body become abnormal, and the second that they divide uncontrollably, the body thus producing large numbers of these abnormal cells.

E) Medical Research

Medical research is conducted to further knowledge about health and disease. It involves a range of methods, of which experiments using animals are a small but controversial part. It is carried out in universities, hospitals and other research establishments, funded by the government, charities and the pharmaceutical industry. This industry also takes forward the fruits of some medical research to enable the development of new drugs. By law, these drugs must be safety tested on at least two species of animal before they enter clinical trials in people.

F) Clinical Trials

Clinical trials evaluate drugs, non-drug treatments or other medical interventions, such as diagnostic methods, in people. The purpose of such trials is to determine whether the treatment or intervention is safe, effective, and, where relevant, better than current standard care. The trials must pass ethical approval, involve the full and informed consent of participating human subjects and are very closely monitored.

G) Viable Alternative

Capable of success or continuing effectiveness; practicable: a viable plan; a viable national economy. In terms of the use of animals in medical research, if there is no viable alternative, then there is no other method that would have as good a chance of achieving the same goal.

H) Vivisection

Dissection of living animals for experimental purposes. The use of the term in recent years has been expanded to include all experimentation on living animals, rather than just dissection alone.

Overview: The use of animals in medical research

Animals are used in medical research for several purposes. About a third of such research is 'basic' or 'fundamental,' aimed at understanding how the body, or its component cells and organs, work. A further third is 'applied,' to increase understanding of and develop new treatments for disease. It includes safety testing of new medicines (required by law; accounts for about 10% of all animal use) and non-drug safety testing (e.g. for agricultural or domestic products). The remaining third includes breeding animals for the increasing number of studies on the genetic basis of health or disease and other relatively small areas such as developing new diagnostic methods.

In 2004, about 85% of animal research involved rats, mice and other rodents. Other animals used very occasionally include dogs and cats (0.3%) and monkeys, such as marmosets and macaques (0.15%). The use of chimpanzees, orangutans and gorillas is banned in the UK, all animals are bred for research (strays/unwanted pets cannot be used) and cosmetic testing was banned here in 1998.

The Animals (Scientific Procedures) Act 1986 regulates scientific procedures which 'may cause pain, suffering, distress or lasting harm' to 'protected animals'. These are: all living non-human vertebrates (animals with backbones or spines) and one invertebrate, the common octopus. A new level of regulation introduced in April 1999, local ethical review, makes the UK the only country where animal research is regulated through both such ethics committees and central government.

UK guiding principles for animal research are called the 'Three Rs,' as they aim to reduce the number of animals used to a minimum, refine the way experiments are carried out to minimise suffering and replace animal experiments with non-animal techniques wherever possible. Opinion polls suggest that while most people would like more alternatives used, they accept using animals in research as long as it is ethical, well-regulated, for medical benefit and minimises suffering, and they abhor the tactics of violent animal rights extremists. There is also evidence that people are more concerned about the use of some animals than others ('speciesism') which leads to questions about whether there are scientific or morally relevant differences between species, such as mice, cats and monkeys?.

The following table summarises some of the main arguments outlined above.

For	Against
Gives useful information about how the body works in health and disease; we share approximately 90% of our DNA with mice	Scientifically misleading: animals and man differ too much, and stressed lab animals give invalid information
Ethically justified, or indeed an ethical imperative, because humans matter more than animals	Morally wrong because it causes suffering to living creatures who can't choose whether or not to participate
Does not always cause suffering: often involves little more than taking tests or making observations	Frequently causes pain and suffering, and deprives animals of a normal life
Stringent regulations safeguard animals and ensure best practice and high welfare standards	Rules are ignored, monitoring is inadequate and undercover investigations reveal animal abuse
Animal research and testing are carried out for scientific reasons	Animal research and testing are commercially-driven, multi-million pound concerns
New medicines have caused death or injury because they were not adequately tested on animals	Many drugs have dangerous side-effects that were not predicted by animal models, and drugs can have different effects in animals and man
Animal health and care have improved as a result of research involving animals	The benefits to animals come at too high a price: we should use existing knowledge, but not do new research

Discussion Trigger 1:

Is it different to test on monkeys and dogs than it is on rats?

> SONNY: We're very concerned about the use of primates in brain research.

The objection to the use of animals in research for some people appears to vary depending on which animals specifically are involved. There appear to be two main justifications for this speciesism:

1 The more like us the animal is (e.g. primates) the higher the level of objection

2 The more attractive in appearance and/or behaviour (e.g. dogs, cats and other animals kept as pets) the higher the level of objection

It is important to understand the numbers of animals from different species that are used: **http://www.rds-online.org.uk/pages/page.asp?i_ToolbarID=2&i_PageID=32**

Issues/Prompts

- What do we mean when we say an animal is more like us?
- Should the appearance of an animal make a difference in whether it is used in medical research? Why?
- Should the intelligence of an animal make a difference to whether it is used in medical research? Why?
- What factors should determine whether an animal is used in medical research?
- Does it make a difference that only a relatively small number of 'higher mammals' are used in medical research?

Some anti-vivisectionists say it is wrong to use animals because they are so like humans. Some anti-vivisectionists say it is wrong to use animals because they are so different the results of animal research are not transferable to humans. Is it possible to hold both these views?

Discussion Trigger 2:

What responsibilities do we have to animals?

> SONNY: It's a farm. They breed dogs there. Experiment dogs. The conditions they keep them in look really bad.
>
> LINA: You sure? I thought they had rules and regulations for that sort of thing.
>
> SONNY: They have, but that doesn't mean people stick to them.

Issues/Prompts

- Why do we have responsibilities towards animals?
- Do animals have rights? What are they? What is a right? Are these the same rights as humans?
- Is it ever right to use animals to serve humans? In what ways do humans use animals? Which of these, if any, do you think are justifiable?
- What are our responsibilities towards:
  - ▲ Domestic animals?

- ▲ Wild animals?
- ▲ Animals used for other human purposes?
- What laws or regulations do we need to ensure these responsibilities are carried out?
- How can we ensure they are carried out?

Discussion Trigger 3:

What rights to protest should people have? What about the right to carry out legal research?

SONNY: Oh. Listen. Kelsey's invited me to a Protest on Wednesday night. Outside this new Animal Research Laboratory they're trying to build in town.

LINA: (*Worried.*) Sonny.

SONNY: It's a peaceful protest. Don't worry.

LINA: Some of these animal rights people are really violent.

Issues/Prompts

- Where do you think Lina gets her view from?
- How does the media tend to present animal rights protesters? Is this fair? Why do the media choose to do this? (See page 122)
- The media's focus on the extreme behaviour of a small minority of animal rights protesters distracts the public from the real issue. Do you agree?
- Why do people protest? In what ways do people protest? Which of these do you think are acceptable and which are unacceptable?
- 'Animal rights protesters using violence are undermining a free and civilized society.' Do you agree?
- New laws make it a criminal offence to cause 'economic damage' (i.e. financial loss) to medical research companies or to protest outside the homes of scientists. An animal rights activist said: 'The government is bringing in laws to protect people who murder animals'. Do you agree?
- What do you think of Sonny's protest in the play? Did he go too far? Or not far enough?

Discussion Trigger 4:

How can the public find out what takes place inside laboratories that conduct experiments on animals?

SONNY: (*To RAZ.*) We've been leafleting in Town, about the Animal Research Laboratory actually. I could give you some information about it if you like.

ANITA: If you like reading unproven propaganda he means.

Part of the issue with being open and transparent about what takes place inside laboratories has come about from the fact that extra security has been put in place to counter destructive protest.

Issues/Prompts

- Do the public have a right to know what goes on in animal research laboratories?
- How can you get hold of truthful information? What sources of information are available?
- How can you ensure you get a balanced perspective?

Discussion Trigger 5:

Some research is aimed at gaining knowledge about how the body works, and may result in helping us better understand illness. Is it still okay to use animals here?

> ANITA: Basic research is about acquiring knowledge. It doesn't have to lead to a cure for something.
>
> SONNY: So then why do it if… [it doesn't?]
>
> ANITA: (*Overlaps.*) Because we need to know. We need to understand.
>
> SONNY: You don't need to know, you just want to know.

Basic research accounts for about one third of animal research in the UK. It increases scientific knowledge about the way humans and animals behave or develop and function biologically. It is not necessarily intended to lead to applications to humans. (Nuffield Report: The Ethics of Research Involving Animals *page 2)*

Issues/Prompts

- What is the value of basic research? What useful outcomes might there be?
- Is it justifiable to use animals in this way when we don't know what the value of the research might be?
- What is the purpose of science?
- Is it ever wrong to limit the quest for knowledge?

Discussion Trigger 6:

Research into life-threatening illness involves some suffering, or the death of, thousands of animals. Is that okay?

> SONNY: So you think it's alright to perform unnecessary operations on defenceless animals who can't say no?
>
> ANITA: Look. If you ever have the misfortune to suffer from a brain disease you'll thank the scientists who've used monkeys for helping you.
>
> SONNY: I'd rather thank the monkeys. How many of them suffered? And died?

Issues

- Is human suffering worse than animal suffering? Why?
- UK legislation allows scientists to cause animals pain, suffering, distress or lasting harm during medical research. Is this justifiable?
- Is human life more important than animal life? Why?

- What can we learn from religious perspectives?
- If research on animals can lead to reducing human suffering, is it ethically right not to do it?

Discussion Trigger 7:

What does the Buddhist perspective teach us?

SONNY: What's the Buddhists' view about Animal Rights?

RAZ: Ah. They say that no living thing should be harmed, if you can help it. We all breathe the same air don't we? Animals and humans. Every breath is precious. Breathing's very important to Buddhists.

Issues
- In what ways do humans use animals?
- Which of these count as harmful?
- Which of these can be avoided?
- Is it possible to live without causing harm to animals?

Discussion Trigger 8:

Is it right to use genetically modified animals in research?

ANITA: The mice used are genetically modified okay. They're created specially for testing Asthma medicines.

SONNY: That doesn't make it okay Anita. Scientists playing God again.

ANITA: It means that they're exactly right for the tests, they get the most accurate results.

SONNY: They just see them as tools, not living breathing animals. Are you saying they deliberately create asthma-suffering mice?

ANITA: Yes.

SONNY: Oh great.

Some animals are genetically modified in order for them to replicate human disease/conditions as closely as possible. The closer the similarity with human illness the more precise the research results which in the long run may reduce the numbers of animals used in medical research. However, in the short term the numbers of animals may increase as they become an improved means of research.

Issues/Prompts
- Is it right to genetically modify animals?
- Is it right to deliberately create diseased animals?
- What does Sonny mean by 'Scientists playing God'?

What if, in the long run, such animals lead to medical breakthroughs in the treatment of humans or animals or a long-term reduction of number of animals used in medical research?

Lesson 1: Initial Responses

Focus

The following are suggestions for how you might pick up on the ideas and issues raised by the play and discuss the students' initial responses. You can select to do one or more from the range below. They can be used as stand alone exercises or as preparation for one of the other lessons. They use a range of strategies and could be used in a variety of different lessons: i.e. PSHE/ Science/English/Drama/Form Tutor Period etc.

If you used the Preparatory Lessons

If you used the Preparatory Lessons 'What Do We Feel?' and 'What Do We Think?' it may be interesting to return to the activities to see how the students' ideas have changed since reading *Every Breath*. (See Preparatory Lessons, 'What do we feel?' and 'What do we think?')

What Do We Think? – An Active Discussion

The Preparatory Lesson 'What Do We Think?' would work as an interesting follow-up exercise regardless of whether it has been done beforehand (see above).

A Discussion Exercise

Divide the students into pairs or small groups. Ask them to discuss and write down their answers to the following questions:

- What did you like/dislike about the play?
- Why do you think the play is called *Every Breath*? Do you think it's a good title?
- What surprised you in the play? What new things did you learn?
- Did anything make you laugh? Was this appropriate in relation to the subject?
- What didn't you understand? What do you need further clarification on?
- What questions has the play made you ask?

After allowing 10 minutes to discuss their answers ask each group to share their answers and discuss them as a whole group.

Still Image Exercise – Memorable moment

Divide the class into groups of four.

Ask the group to share with each other the moment of the play that sticks most strongly in their mind.

Each group must agree on one of these moments and create a still image of that moment (not all the group members have to be in the image).

Share the images with the class.

Try and identify each one and discuss the different choices. Is there a consensus about the most memorable moment? What made it memorable?

Still Image Exercise – Capturing the essence
Divide the class into groups of four.

Ask them to create a still image that captures the 'essence' of the play (this demands that they have a good discussion between themselves about what they think the play was about).

Share and discuss the different ideas. Are any more accurate or do they just represent different views about what is important?

Practical Exercise – Telling the Story
Divide the class into groups of four.

Ask them to tell the story as succinctly and accurately as possible in one of the following ways:

- Freeze Frames (max. 5)
- Sentences (max. 8)
- Improvisation (max. 1 min)

Share and discuss the differences between the versions.

Lesson 2: Science Regulating Research

Focus
To understand how research using animals is regulated in the UK by simulating a research licence application procedure.

Objectives
To weigh up the necessity of using animals for a specific piece of research.

To explore the possibility of using non-animal research methods.

To gain an understanding of UK regulations governing research using animals.

National Curriculum Links
SCIENCE KS4 4a & b

Resources
Information Sheet 1: How research using animals is regulated
Information Sheet 2: Your research
Information Sheet 3: The 'Three Rs'

Activity

1) Divide the class into groups of three to six and give them the following brief:

   The optic nerve connects the eye to the brain, carrying the electrical impulses which enable us to see. You are a team of research scientists trying to discover whether it's possible to reconnect a severed optic nerve. Finding this out could have many uses: reversing accidental damage to this nerve, which can cause blindness, giving clues for reversing other types of blindness and possibly even treating people with spinal cord injuries. The research would involve rats.

   In order to be allowed to do your research you have to apply for a licence.

2) Distribute *Information Sheet 1: How research using animals is regulated* (page 100), and ask students to read.

3) Give the students the following information:

   Each member of your team has a **Personal Licence** and the place where you are carrying out your research has a **Research Facility Licence**. You now need to put together your case to apply for your Project Licence.

   Distribute *Information Sheet 2: Your research* (page 102) and *Information Sheet 3: The 'Three Rs'* (page 103). Ask students to read *Information Sheet 2: Your research*, in order to understand the research they want to carry out. They should keep *Information Sheet 3: The 'Three Rs'* for reference for the following exercise.

4) Ask students to discuss the following in their groups:
   a Is your research important enough to justify the use of animals? (i.e. Do the likely benefits of the research outweigh the costs to animals?)
   b Can you think of ways of carrying out your research without using animals? (Look at *Information Sheet 3: The 'Three Rs'* – 'Replacement'.)
   c Will your work 'translate' from rats into man?

(Feedback)

5) In order to apply for your Project Licence you need to be able to demonstrate how your research implements the Three Rs. Read *Information Sheet 3: The 'Three Rs'* and in your group discuss and note down your answers to the following questions:

Reduction – How do you intend to keep the number of animals used to a minimum?

Refinement – How will you ensure your experiment is carried out in such a way to ensure animal suffering is minimised?

Replacement – Could you use non-animal methods?

(Feedback)

Possible Extension Exercise

If appropriate this work could be developed into a written exercise titled Application to the Home Secretary for a Research Project Licence, with answers written under the following headings:

a What is the research you want to do?

b Justify why it is necessary to use animals.

c Explain how you are going to keep the number of animals used to a minimum.

d Explain how you are going to keep suffering to a minimum.

e Explain why you can't use non-animal methods.

Information Sheet 1 – How research using animals is regulated (Science)

The UK has a long tradition of protecting animals and this is especially true of animals used in research. There have been special controls on the use of laboratory animals in the UK since 1876.

In 1986 the laws governing the use of animals in research were extended and revised to ensure that the welfare of the animals was safeguarded while allowing important medical research to continue.

The resulting Animals (Scientific Procedures) Act is widely recognised as the strictest in the world. This UK Act will only allow research to be carried out using animals if any benefit the research is likely to bring outweighs any pain and distress the animals may suffer.

More detailed information on the 1986 Act can be found on the Home Office Web site at **http://www.homeoffice.gov.uk/animact/**.

What scientists have to do before they are allowed to carry out research using animals – The Project Licence

Three licences are required for any scientific work using animals under the 1986 Act.

1) THE PROJECT LICENCE

If a scientist wants to carry out research or testing using animals they must first obtain a Project Licence from the Home Secretary who will take advice from the inspectorate in the first instance before granting the licence.

The licence will only be granted if:

- The results of the research are likely to be important enough to justify the use of animals
- The research cannot be done without using animals
- Any suffering is kept to an absolute minimum
- Monkeys, dogs and cats are only used when no other species, usually rodents, are suitable
- The people working with animals have undergone training and testing on the species of animal they wish to use, the type of procedure they are going to carry out and the level of distress the animal may suffer

The scientists have shown that they have, as far as possible:

- Reduced the number of animals used to a minimum.
- Refined the way the experiment is carried out to make sure that any animal suffering is minimised
- Replaced the use of animals with non-animal methods wherever possible

These three principles, Reduce, Refine and Replace, are called the 'Three Rs' and are the guiding principles in animal research

More information can be found at **http://www.rds-online.org.uk/welfare/threers** and **http://www.nc3rs.org.uk/**.

2) THE PERSONAL LICENCE

The person actually carrying out the research on the animal must first obtain a personal licence by attending the appropriate training courses and passing the relevant examinations. They must be qualified to:

- Work on a particular species of animal
- Carry out the specific procedure required
- Work only to the levels of suffering for the animals laid down in the project licence. The suffering is classed as mild, moderate or severe. Very few procedures involving severe levels of suffering are allowed in the UK

3) THE RESEARCH FACILITY LICENCE

The research must be carried out in an approved research facility which will have been inspected and shown that:

- It has accommodation for the animals that meets the required standards
- Has vets on call 24 hours a day

If the facility meets these very rigorous standards then it is given a Certificate of Designation.

Many additions have been made to the Act since 1986 to make it even more stringent. The latest was added in April 1999 and this new regulation means that a project must now pass through an additional local ethical review before a licence is granted.

Adapted from Biomedical Research Educational Trust (BRET) website: Information on Animal Welfare and the laws governing Animal Research http://www.bret.org.uk/gov.htm

Information Sheet 2 – Your research (Science)

You want to carry out research to see if it's possible to re-connect a severed optic nerve – the nerve which carries signals from the eye to the brain, enabling us to see. If successful, your research could help to restore sight, and might also give us clues about how to repair other sorts of damage to the brain, nerves or spinal cord. Your research would involve severing the optic nerve in rats, rejoining them, and looking at ways to encourage them to grow normally again. Following this surgery, you would study the rats over a period of months to assess this.

(For further detail see: **http://www.rdsonline.org.uk/pages/headline_detail. asp?i_ToolbarID=6&i_PageID=771**)

Structure of the Eye

The Optic Nerve

The **Optic Nerve**

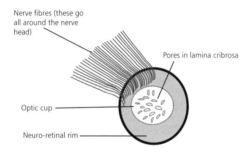

Nerve fibres (these go all around the nerve head)

Pores in lamina cribrosa

Optic cup

Neuro-retinal rim

Structure of the **optic nerve** head (head on)

Behind the **pupil**, the **lens** of the eye is suspended from the **ciliary body** by fine ligaments. The **cornea** and **lens** focus a picture of your surroundings on the **retina**, which is the light-sensitive layer that coats the inside of the eye. The picture of your surroundings is sent from the **retina** to the brain by nerve fibres, which derive from nerve cells in the **retina**. The **optic nerve** is formed by about one million of these nerve fibres collected together. The **optic nerve** starts at the back of the eye at the **optic nerve** head, which is also called the **optic disc**.

The nerve fibres leave the eye through pores (holes) in the **lamina cribrosa**, a sieve-like structure in the optic nerve head. Blood vessels enter and leave the eye through the same structure. The nerve fibres form a rim around the edge of the **optic nerve** head (**neuro-retinal** rim), leaving a central indentation without nerve fibres called the **optic cup**.

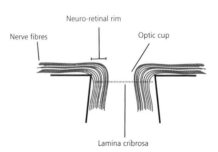

Neuro-retinal rim

Nerve fibres

Optic cup

Lamina cribrosa

Structure of the **optic nerve** head (side on)

http://www.glaucoma-association.com/nqcontent.cfm?a_id=340&=fromcfc&tt= article&lang=en&site_id=176

Information Sheet 3 – The 'Three Rs' (Science)

The principles of the Three Rs – Replacement, Refinement and Reduction – were developed as criteria for humane animal use in research and testing.

Replacement

Replacement refers to the use of non-animal methods instead of animals to achieve a scientific aim. Safety testing is probably the area where most progress has been made in the development of direct replacements for animals.

The non-animal techniques are:

- **in vitro techniques**, involving the study of isolated molecules, cells and tissues (which may come from humans, animals, micro-organisms or even plants). This gives useful information about interactions between molecules, within or between cells, or about organ function.
- **study of human beings and populations.** Research on human subjects can give very useful information about the body in health and disease, and about the distribution of diseases in society, but is limited by what is considered ethical. New non-invasive scanning techniques make it possible to study blood flow or nerve activity in the living human brain, for instance.
- **Computers** and chemical techniques can screen out harmful or useless compounds before they ever get to the animal testing stage.
- **Genetic studies** are a growing area of research, and may be carried out at molecular and cellular levels. But they often lead directly to the use of more animals, to study the effect of particular genetic changes in living beings.
- **Microdosing** is a new method being developed. It involves giving human subjects a drug dose one-hundredth of what would be necessary for it to have an actual effect on the body and watching what the body does with it. With the aid of accelerator mass spectometry (AMS) — an incredibly sensitive measuring technique, which can pick up minute traces of a drug in the human body — the metabolic fate of a drug administered in trace doses can be followed. It may allow scientists to watch the metabolism of new drugs in the human body with no risk. (*The Times*: 'The Human Guinea Pigs', 17/12/05 **http://www.curedisease.net/articles/051217.shtml**)

Refinement

Refinement refers to methods which alleviate or minimise potential pain, suffering or distress, and which enhance animal welfare, for those animals which still have to be used. Refinement can be achieved by, for example, using appropriate anaesthetics, training animals to co-operate with certain procedures (e.g. taking blood samples) so the animals are less stressed, and ensuring that accommodation meets the animals' needs (e.g. providing opportunities for nesting for rodents). There is evidence that refinement not only benefits the animals, but also improves the quality of the research findings.

The 'mouse house' is a refinement developed at the MRC National Institute for Medical Research. The transparent, red, plastic house provides mice with an area to nest, hide and climb. The mouse house appears dark to the mice as they cannot see red, yet the transparent walls mean that animal care staff can see the mice at all times and so are able to carry out their daily checks without disturbing them.

Reduction

Reduction refers to methods which enable researchers to obtain comparable levels of information from fewer animals, or to obtain more information from the same number of animals. Improved experimental design and statistical analysis are means of achieving reduction. The National Centre for Three Rs recently awarded a prize to a scientist who developed a way of reducing the number of animals used in a specific piece of research:

In her research, Dr Wiles infects mice with bacteria from the same family as *E coli* to study the paths of infection. Traditionally, every mouse has been infected by putting a tube down its throat to deliver the bacteria to the stomach – a process called gavage. Dr Wiles tried infecting only one mouse in this way, then putting it in a cage with uninfected mice and letting nature take its course. The results showed higher infection rates than the traditional technique. But more importantly, the research was refined so that far fewer animals were subjected to gavage, and the new approach also reduced the total number of animals used by improving the reliability of infection.

Adapted from

The National Centre for the Three Rs website:

The Three Rs: **http://www.nc3rs.org.uk/page.asp?id=7**

The NC3Rs Prize: **http://www.nc3rs.org.uk/page.asp?id=149**

The RDS website:

Non-Animal Research Methods:
http://www.rds-online.org.uk/pages/page.asp?i_ToolbarID=2&i_PageID=33
http://www.rds-online.org.uk/pages/page.asp?i_ToolbarID=4&i_PageID=148

Lesson 3: Drama
What do the characters learn?

Aim
To explore how the characters learn and change over the course of the play.

Objectives
To understand the inter-connection between relationships and views.

To understand that personal views may change in relation to other people and events.

To demonstrate how the characters' relationships and views change over the course of the play.

National Curriculum Links
PSHE KS3 3g, h & I KS4 3e
ENGLISH (Drama) KS3 & KS4 4a & b

Resources
Play Synopsis.
Possibly white board and pen.

Activity
1   Divide the class into groups of four. Ask them to tell the story of EVERY BREATH as succinctly and accurately as possible in one of the following ways (you may like to refer to the play synopsis in Preparatory Lessons to help you):
    • Freeze Frames (max. 7)
    • Freeze Frames with captions (max. 5)
    • Speed improvisation (max. time 1 min)

    Share and discuss the differences between the versions.

2   Ask the students to create a series of four freeze-frames of the relationships between the four characters at the following moments of the play. The aim is to capture how the relationships change:
    • At the start of the play i.e. before Anita comes home from University
    • Mid-way through the meal scene before Sonny has his Asthma attack
    • After Anita's visit to the hospital
    • The end of the play

    (It may also be interesting to include one of the family before the start of the play when the father was still alive, i.e. to introduce the idea of how his death has affected the views and relationships of individuals within the family. The person previously playing Raz could play the father.)

3   Extension Exercise

    You could ask the groups to 'morph' their freeze-frames into each other i.e. show the transition from one freeze-frame to the next as a slow merging process. Can they do this in such a way as to teach us something further about the changing relationships?

4   Watch the groups and use this as a springboard to discuss how the
    characters change over the course of the play. Why? What do they each
    learn?

    If you intend to continue to the next exercise it may be useful to note down
    the ideas that are suggested for Anita and Sonny.

5   Extension Exercise

    Divide the class into pairs. Each pair can choose whether they want to work
    on the character of Sonny or Anita.

    In their pairs they must work on the following role-plays/missing scenes
    from the story. The focus is to demonstrate how the characters change over
    the play, and thus one scene is near the start and one towards the end of
    the play:

    SONNY

    1   Sonny and Kelsey (his girlfriend)/or a friend

        When: After Scene 3 – Saturday morning, his conversation with Anita
        over breakfast

        Things to include:

        Sonny's attitude towards Anita

        Sonny's attitude to taking his Asthma medication

    2   Sonny and Kelsey

        When: At the end of the play

        Things to include:

        Sonny's attitude towards Anita

        Sonny's attitude to taking his Asthma medication

    ANITA

    1   Anita and her boyfriend/a friend

        When: After Scene 3 – Saturday morning, her conversation with Sonny
        over breakfast

        Things to include:

        Anita's attitude to Sonny's new job on the pussy cat van and his decision
        to stop taking his Asthma medication

    2   Anita and her boyfriend/a friend

        When: At the end of the play

        Things to include:

        Anita's attitude towards Sonny (the seriousness with which he holds his
        view) and her own attitude towards her research

    Allow 10–15 minutes for the pairs to work on their scenes.

    Then watch some and comment on anything new you have discovered
    about what the characters learnt.

    What have you learnt from doing this exercise?

Lesson 4: Drama – Sonny's Dilemmas

Aim

To consider the factors that influence Sonny's decision to stop taking and then re-take his asthma medication.

Objectives

To understand the ethical and scientific arguments involved in Sonny's decision.

To understand the influence of relationships and emotional factors in Sonny's decision.

To vocalise those factors through role-play and improvisation.

National Curriculum Links

PSHE: KS3 3b, 4g and KS4 1a, 2b, 4g
ENGLISH (Drama): KS3 & KS4 4a, 4b

Activity

1   Some time before the start of the play, Sonny has faced a big decision:

Should he or should he not take asthma medication which has been tested on animals?

He has decided to stop using his inhaler and taking his steroids, risking both deterioration in his general condition and increasing the danger of an asthma attack.

Discuss:

What are his reasons for making this decision? How do you think his relationships have influenced his decision? (i.e. Kelsey, Anita, his Dad, his Mum, someone at Animal Kind.)

2   Divide the class into pairs and ask each pair to choose one of the above characters who they think has influenced Sonny's decision. Ask them to create a scene which demonstrates this.

Show and discuss which influences are the most significant.

3   Although he doesn't admit it at the time, Sonny's decision at the end of the play to take the medication again indicates he was re-assessing the situation in hospital. What factors do think influenced his change of mind? (Think about his conversations with his Mum, Anita and Raz and any other factors you think important)

4   Conscience Alley

Ask a volunteer to represent Sonny. Ask the other students to form two lines facing each other with Sonny standing at one end. The students should be facing Sonny.

Tell the students they are going to be speaking the thoughts in Sonny's head as he is deciding whether to re-take his medication (it is almost a physical representation of his journey home from hospital). He will probably have conflicting thoughts going though his mind. Ask each person in the line to think of a thought that might influence Sonny's decision.

Ask Sonny to walk down the alley between the two lines of students. As he passes each student they should speak their line.

When Sonny has reached the end ask what he would do as a result of what he's just heard. Discuss as a group what they think the most significant influences are.

6 Impro

Divide the class into pairs: Sonny and Kelsey

Scene: Sonny tells Kelsey about the decision he has made to re-take his asthma drugs.

How does she react? How does he feel explaining it to her? You may need to discuss what her attitude is like towards animal testing and whether he should take the drugs. You could try the scene in two ways:

1   She is strongly against Sonny backing down and thinks he should continue his protest. Perhaps she isn't very understanding about what he's been through. Can Sonny persuade her?

2   She is very supportive of Sonny's decision but surprised by his change of mind. She wonders what's changed?

Discuss further what you learn about Sonny's decision.

Lesson 5: PHSE
Challenging Stereotypes

This lesson is primarily a PSHE lesson which uses drama techniques. However, it can be adapted to have a stronger Drama focus by making it a comparison between stereotypes and complex characters.

Aim
To explore and understand the differences between stereotypes and complex individuals.

Objectives
To create dramatic representations of stereotypes and complex characters.

To understand why stereotypes arise.

To understand the limitations of stereotyping.

National Curriculum Links
PSHE KS3 3a, KS4 3c
ENGLISH (Drama) KS3 & KS4 4a & b

Resources
Large Empty Classroom/Drama studio
White board. Marker pen.

Activities

1   Warm-up Game – Exploring social stereotypes

    Pupils stand in a circle. Explain to them that in a moment they are going to face outwards and you are going to say a word to which they will have three seconds to create a physical representation and then turn in to face the group.

    Use words from the following list. After each, count aloud to three and ask the pupils to turn in making their physical representation. They can have a brief look at each other's and then turn back out and wait for the next word.

    Actor   Teenager   Student   Mother   Father   Tourist
    American   Rugby Player   Italian   Preacher   Brit   Football Player
    Politician   Celebrity

    Make the point that most of these images will have drawn upon stereotypes that we each hold about many people in society.

2   Make the point that at the start of the play each of the characters hold stereotypical views of each other and individuals involved in the animal experimentation debate. Ask if anyone can remember what any of these views were.

    Ask pupils to stand in a space. Read out the following quotes from the play and ask them to create a physical representation of the stereotype the words suggest.

Animal Rights Activists

LINA: Some of these Animal Rights People are really violent.

ANITA: The Pussy Cat Van! What is that? Poor ickle pussy cats! Are these people still at nursery school? Why don't they call animals by their proper names?

ANITA: If you like reading unproven propaganda he means.

Scientists

SONNY: Yeah. More boffins like yourself. What do you talk about? Scientific formulas?

RAZ: Meeting in secret to conduct dastardly experiments!

SONNY: You just want to go on doing your 'interesting work' like all the other scientists. You don't want to think about the animals because thinking about the animals means you'd have to stop.

SONNY: You think science is all about being definite, all about being right.

Buddhists

ANITA: Has he got a shaved head and love beads?

Discuss how far these stereotypes are a fair representation of the characters in the play?

3 Write the name of each character on a board. As a whole class, brainstorm all the details you can remember about each character. Pay particular attention to things that challenge the stereotype or contradict other aspects of their character.

4 Divide the class into small groups of three to five. Allocate one of the four characters to each group (or you could just choose to focus on Sonny and Anita).

   Ask the group to create a multi-faceted image for their character, i.e. a group image which reflects different aspects of the character, perhaps with each person representing a different facet.

5 Each person should think of a line they can say which adds further detail to their character.

6 Show and discuss:
   - Why do we create stereotypes?
   - How truthful are they?
   - What is the impact of stereotyping?
   - Is stereotyping something to be avoided? How can we?

Lesson 6: RE
What do the major religions have to say?

Aim
To explore and understand what the major religions say about the relative values of animal and human life and the use of animals for medical research.

Objectives
To learn about what the different religious viewpoints are.

To voice a particular religious viewpoint as if it is your own.

To understand how a religious viewpoint might influence someone making a decision about using medication tested on animals.

To understand the value of religious viewpoints in the wider debate about animals in medical research.

National Curriculum Links
RE: KS3: 1a & e. 3i, j, k, o & p KS4 1a, 2a, b & c

Resources
Play Extracts: *Scene 7 – Hospital*
Information Sheet – Religious views

Discussion Starter
The character of Raz in *Every Breath* is 'thinking about becoming a Buddhist.'

How does this affect his view on animals?

What impact does this have on Sonny and his decision about whether or not to take his Asthma medication?

You might like to look at Play Extracts: *Scene 7 – Hospital* to refresh your memory.

Activity
1   Divide the class into pairs. Distribute *Information Sheet – Religious views* and allocate to each pair one of the major religions to focus on.

2   Ask the pair to read the information for the religion they have been allocated and note down the major points about that religion's view of:
   a   the way animals should be treated
   b   the value of animal life in relation to human life
   c   experiments on animals

3   Role-Play

   Ask the pairs to label themselves A and B and give them the following information:

   A is a friend of Sonny's who holds the religious faith/or is in the process of considering the religious faith they have just been studying.

   B is Sonny, in hospital considering whether or not he should take his Asthma medication.

   A comes to visit Sonny in hospital. Sonny asks, 'What's your view about Animal Rights?'

Ask them to role-play the scene. They should aim to make the scene:

- a realistic portrayal of a conversation between two friends and informative to the rest of the class about the view of the religion they are representing.

They might like to discuss beforehand the kinds of things A might say. They should bear in mind that most of the religions do not have a clear-cut right or wrong view, so they should simply select some ideas from the information given.

After letting the scene run for two to three minutes, ask them to review how it went and re-run bearing in mind their two aims.

4   Ask representatives from each religion to present their scene to the rest of the class.

After each one discuss:

a   What were the religious ideas presented?

b   What impact did the conversation have on Sonny?

Extension Activity

5   An Independent Ethics Committee advises the Government about whether or not certain experiments involving animals should be allowed.

Discuss:

Do you think representatives from the major religions should have a place on such a committee? Why?/Why not?

What other voices should be represented?

As a class draw up a list of who you think should be represented on the Independent Ethics Committee.

6   You can either run this exercise as a whole class or in small groups of five to six. Present them with the following scenario:

You are the independent Ethics Committee deciding if the research that Anita wants to do in the play, researching mice in the new lab, should be allowed (we are taking a step back in time here in the imaginary world of the play).

Anita's research involves examining mice to discover more about how the genes in their hearts and livers work at different times of the day. As part of this work, the mice are killed, and their organs removed. This type of research is known as basic research and its purpose is to gain knowledge about how the body works. It is not directly linked to a particular illness, but its outcomes may lead to improvements in medicine or care further down the line.

Using the religious views considered earlier in the lesson, debate whether or not you think the research should go ahead.

If done in small groups, feedback the main points discussed in your debate to the rest of the class.

Information Sheet – Religious Views (RE Lesson)

Judaism

The way Jews should treat animals is encapsulated in Proverbs 12:10: 'The righteous person regards the life of his beast'.

Judaism teaches that animals are part of God's creation and should be treated with compassion. Human beings must avoid 'tzar baalei chayim' – causing pain to any living creature. God himself makes a covenant with the animals, just as he does with humanity. The Talmud specifically instructs Jews not to cause pain to animals, and there are also several Bible stories which use kindness to animals as a demonstration of the virtues of leading Jewish figures.

Judaism also teaches that it is acceptable to harm or kill animals if that is the only way to fulfill an essential human need. This is because people take priority over animals, something stated very early in the Bible, where God gives human beings the right to control all non-human animals. Human beings are therefore allowed to use animals for food and clothing – and to provide parchment on which to write the Bible.

Scripture and animals

'And God blessed Noah and his sons, and said unto them, be fruitful, and multiply, and replenish the earth.

'And the fear of you and the dread of you shall be upon every beast of the earth, and upon every fowl of the air, upon all that moveth upon the earth, and upon all the fishes of the sea; into your hand are they delivered.

'Every moving thing that liveth shall be meat for you; even as the green herb have I given you all things.' (Genesis 9: 1-3.)

Genesis, the first book of the Bible, states that God has given human beings dominion over all living things. Dominion is interpreted as stewardship – living things are to serve humanity but human beings, as part of their dominion, are required to look after all living creatures.

'His tender mercies are over all His creatures' (Psalm 145:9)

The Bible gives several instructions on animal welfare:

- A person must feed his animals before himself (Deuteronomy 11:15)
- Animals must be allowed to rest on the Sabbath (Exodus 20:10 & Deuteronomy 5: 14)
- An animal's suffering must be relieved (Deuteronomy 12:4)

Jews are instructed to avoid:

- Severing a limb from a live animal and eating it (Genesis 9:4)
- Killing a cow and her calf on the same day (Leviticus 22:28) – this demonstrates that Judaism accepts that animals have powerful family relationships)
- Muzzling an animal threshing corn (Deuteronomy 25:4)
- Harnessing an ox and donkey together (Deuteronomy 22:10)

Experiments on animals

Jewish teaching allows animal experiments as long both of these conditions are satisfied:

- There is a real possibility of a benefit to human beings
- There is no unnecessary pain involved

Islam

> *'There is not an animal on earth, nor a bird that flies on its wings, but they are communities like you…'* Qur'an 6:38

Muslims believe that:

- all living creatures were made by Allah
- Allah loves all animals
- animals exist for the benefit of human beings
- animals must be treated with kindness and compassion

Muslims are instructed to avoid:

- treating animals cruelly
- over-working or over-loading animals
- neglecting animals
- hunting animals for sport
- hunting for food is permitted if the animals are killed humanely
- cutting the mane or tail of a horse
- animal fighting as a sport
- factory farming

Using animals is permitted

The Qur'an explicitly states that animals can be used for human benefit.

> *'It is God who provided for you all manner of livestock, that you may ride on some of them and from some you may derive your food. And other uses in them for you to satisfy your heart's desires. It is on them, as on ships, that you make your journeys.'* Qur'an 40: 79,80

Muhammad (pbuh) and animals

There are many stories and sayings of the Prophet (pbuh) that demonstrate his concern for the welfare of animals. Once someone traveling with the Prophet (pbuh) took some eggs from a nest, causing the mother bird great grief. The Prophet (pbuh) saw this and told the man to return the eggs.

When the Prophet (pbuh), was asked if Allah rewarded acts of charity to animals, he replied: 'Yes, there is a reward for acts of charity to every beast alive'.

The Prophet (pbuh) said: 'Whoever kills a sparrow or anything bigger than that without a just cause, Allah will hold him accountable on the Day of Judgment.' The Prophet explained that a killing would be for a just cause if it was for food.

Experiments on animals

According to Al Hafiz B A Masri, using animals for research may be permitted in Islam. The animals must not suffer pain or mutilation and there must be a good reason for the experiment:

'Actions shall be judged according to intention. Any kind of medical treatment of animals and experiments on them becomes ethical and legal or unethical and illegal according to the intention of the person who does it.' Masri, B.A., Al-Hafiz. *Animals in Islam*. Great Britain: Athene Trust. 1989

Christianity

Introduction
For most of history Christians largely ignored animal suffering. Christian thinkers believed that human beings were greatly superior to animals. They taught that human beings could treat animals as badly as they wanted to because people had few (if any) moral obligations towards animals. Modern Christians generally take a much more pro-animal line. They think that any unnecessary mistreatment of animals is both sinful and morally wrong.

The traditional Christian view
When early theologians looked at 'nature red in tooth and claw' they concluded that it was a natural law of the universe that animals should be preyed on and eaten by others. This was reflected in their theology.

Christian thinking downgraded animals for three main reasons:
1. God had created animals for the use of human beings and human beings were therefore entitled to use them in any way they want
2. Animals were distinctively inferior to human beings and were worth little if any moral consideration, because:
   - humans have souls and animals don't
   - humans have reason and animals don't
3. Christian thought was heavily humano-centric and only considered animals in relation to human beings, and not on their own terms

Animals and saints
Not all leading Christians disparaged animals. Some of the saints demonstrated that virtuous Christians treated animals respectfully and kindly:
- St Antony of Padua preached to fishes
- St Francis of Assisi preached to the birds and became the most popular pro-animal Christian figure
- Cows are protected by St Brigit

Modern Christian thinking about animals
Modern Christian thinking is largely sympathetic to animals and less willing to accept that there is an unbridgeable gap between animals and human beings. Although most theologians don't accept that animals have rights, they do acknowledge that some animals display sufficient consciousness and self-awareness to deserve moral consideration.

The growth of the environmental movement has also radically changed Christian ideas about the role human beings play in relation to nature. Few Christians nowadays think that nature exists to serve humanity, and there is a general acceptance that human dominion over nature should be seen as stewardship and partnership rather than domination and exploitation.

This has significantly softened Christian attitudes to animals.

Animal-friendly Christian thoughts

Here are some of the animal-friendly ideas that modern Christians use when thinking about animals:

- The Bible shows that God made his covenant with animals as well as human beings
- Human and non-human animals have the same origin in God
- St. Francis of Assisi said that animals 'had the same source as himself'
- In God's ideal world human beings live in harmony with animals
  - ▲ The Garden of Eden, in which human beings lived in peace and harmony with animals, demonstrates God's ideal world, and the state of affairs that human beings should work towards
  - ▲ The prophet Isaiah describes the Kingdom of Heaven as a place where animals and human beings live together in peace
- God has the right to have everything he created treated respectfully – wronging animals is wronging God
- God is not indifferent to anything in his creation
- The example of a loving creator God should lead human beings to act lovingly towards animals
  - ▲ Inflicting pain on any living creature is incompatible with living in a Christ-like way
  - ▲ Animals are weak compared to us – Christ tells us to be kind to them
  - ▲ Jesus told human beings to be kind to the weak and helpless
  - ▲ In comparison to human beings, animals are often weak and helpless
  - ▲ Christians should therefore show compassion to animals
- To love those who cannot love you in the same way is a unique way of acting with generous love.
- 'If you love them that love you, what reward have you?'
- It is a great good to take responsibility for the welfare of others, including animals

What the churches say about animals

The Anglican view

This resolution from the 1998 Lambeth Conference of the Anglican Church is typical of contemporary Christian thinking about animals:

> This conference reaffirms the biblical vision of creation according to which Creation is a web of inter-dependent relationships bound together in the covenant which God the Holy Trinity has established with the whole earth and every living being. The divine Spirit is sacramentally present in creation, which is therefore to be treated with reverence, respect and gratitude. Human beings are both co-partners with the rest of creation and living bridges between heaven and earth, with responsibility to make personal & corporate sacrifices for the common good of all creation. The redemptive purpose of God in Jesus Christ extends to the whole of creation.

The Roman Catholic view

The Papal Encyclical 'Evangelium Vitae' recognises that animals have both an intrinsic value and a place in God's kingdom.

The Roman Catholic Ethic of Life, if fully accepted, would lead Christians to avoid anything that brings unnecessary suffering or death to animals.

The official position of the Church is contained in a number of sections of the Church's official Catechism (the paragraphing within each section is ours):

373 In God's plan man and woman have the vocation of 'subduing' the earth as stewards of God.

This sovereignty is not to be an arbitrary and destructive domination. God calls man and woman, made in the image of the Creator 'who loves everything that exists', to share in his providence toward other creatures; hence their responsibility for the world God has entrusted to them.

2415 The seventh commandment enjoins respect for the integrity of creation.

Animals, like plants and inanimate beings, are by nature destined for the common good of past, present, and future humanity.

Use of the mineral, vegetable, and animal resources of the universe cannot be divorced from respect for moral imperatives.

Man's dominion over inanimate and other living beings granted by the Creator is not absolute; it is limited by concern for the quality of life of his neighbour, including generations to come; it requires a religious respect for the integrity of creation.

2416 Animals are God's creatures. He surrounds them with his providential care. By their mere existence they bless him and give him glory.

Thus men owe them kindness. We should recall the gentleness with which saints like St Francis of Assisi or St Philip Neri treated animals.

2417 God entrusted animals to the stewardship of those whom he created in his own image. Hence it is legitimate to use animals for food and clothing. They may be domesticated to help man in his work and leisure.

Medical and scientific experimentation on animals is a morally acceptable practice if it remains within reasonable limits and contributes to caring for or saving human lives.

2418 It is contrary to human dignity to cause animals to suffer or die needlessly.

It is likewise unworthy to spend money on them that should as a priority go to the relief of human misery.

One can love animals; one should not direct to them the affection due only to persons.

Some writers have criticised the statements above for being so firmly centred on human beings. Causing animals to suffer needlessly, for example, is described in 2418 as being contrary to human dignity, rather than as being a wrong towards animals.

Buddhism
Although Buddhism is one of the most animal-friendly religions, some aspects of the tradition are surprisingly negative about animals.

The positive
- Buddhists try to do no harm (or as little harm as possible) to animals

- Buddhists try to show loving-kindness to all beings, including animals
- The doctrine of right livelihood teaches Buddhists to avoid any work connected with the killing of animals
- The doctrine of karma teaches that any wrong behaviour will have to be paid for in a future life – so cruel acts to animals should be avoided

Buddhists treat the lives of human and non-human animals with equal respect. Buddhists see human and non-human animals as closely related:

- both have Buddha-nature
- both have the possibility of becoming perfectly enlightened
- a soul may be reborn either in a human body or in the body of a non-human animal

Buddhists believe that is wrong to hurt or kill animals, because all beings are afraid of injury and death:

All living things fear being beaten with clubs.
All living things fear being put to death.
Putting oneself in the place of the other,
Let no one kill nor cause another to kill. (Dhammapada 129)

The negative

Buddhist behaviour towards and thinking about animals is not always positive. The doctrine of karma implies that souls are reborn as animals because of past misdeeds. Being reborn as an animal is a serious spiritual setback. Because non-human animals can't engage in conscious acts of self-improvement they can't improve their karmic status, and their souls must continue to be reborn as animals until their bad karma is exhausted. Only when they are reborn as human beings can they resume the quest for nirvana.

This bad karma, and the animal's inability to do much to improve it, led Buddhists in the past to think that non-human animals were inferior to human beings and so were entitled to fewer rights than human beings. Early Buddhists (but not the Buddha himself) used the idea that animals were spiritually inferior as a justification for the exploitation and mistreatment of animals.

Experimenting on animals

Buddhists say that this is morally wrong if the animal concerned might come to any harm. However, Buddhists also acknowledge the value that animal experiments may have for human health. So perhaps a Buddhist approach to experiments on animals might require the experimenter to:

- accept the karma of carrying out the experiment
- the experimenter will acquire bad karma through experimenting on an animal
- experiment only for a good purpose
- experiment only on animals where there is no alternative
- design the experiment to do as little harm as possible
- avoid killing the animal unless it is absolutely necessary
- treat the animals concerned kindly and respectfully
- The bad karmic consequences for the experimenter seem to demand a high level of altruistic behaviour in research laboratories

Buddhism and vegetarianism

Not all Buddhists are vegetarian and the Buddha does not seem to have issued an overall prohibition on meat-eating. The Mahayana tradition was (and is) more strictly vegetarian than other Buddhist traditions.

The early Buddhist monastic code banned monks from eating meat if the animal had been killed specifically to feed them, but otherwise instructed them to eat anything they were given.

Hinduism
Because Hinduism is a term that includes many different although related religious ideas, there is no clear single Hindu view on the right way to treat animals, so what follows are generalisations to which there are exceptions.
- The doctrine of ahimsa leads Hindus to treat animals well
- Most Hindus are vegetarian
- No Hindu will eat beef
- Butchery and related jobs are restricted to people of low caste
- Most Hindus believe that non-human animals are inferior to human beings
- Cows are sacred to Hindus
- Some Hindu temples keep sacred animals
- Some Hindu gods have animal characteristics:
  - ▲ Ganesh has the head of an elephant
  - ▲ Hanuman takes the form of a monkey

Animal sacrifice
Hinduism permits animal sacrifice.

Cows
The cow is greatly revered by Hindus and is regarded as sacred. Killing cows is banned in India and no Hindu would eat any cow product.

Taken from BBC Website – Religion and Ethics **http://www.bbc.co.uk/religion/ethics/animals/index**

Lesson 7: English
Looking at Language

Aim
To explore how language is used in the animals in medical research debate to affect a particular response in the reader.

Objectives
To identify examples emotive and objective language.

To understand the different impacts of emotive and objective language.

To write an article using either emotive or objective language.

National Curriculum Links
ENGLISH (Reading) KS3 1a, 4a, 4b, 4c, 4d

Resources
Information Sheet: Articles (page 122)

Activity
1   In the play, Sonny and Anita argue over whether a procedure used on animals during research is 'force' or 'restraint'.

Read out extract below:

ANITA: Okay. (*Reading.*) 'For asthma research we use the mouse inhalation routes, which can be the whole body, or the nose only. Whole body is done in a special chamber. Nose only requires the animals to be restrained with plastic tubes.'

SONNY: So. They basically force themselves to inhale asthma drugs to see if it harms them?

ANITA: To see what the effects are, not just if it harms them. And force isn't the right word.

SONNY: Excuse me, 'restrained with plastic tubes'? They tie them down, they make them asthmatic so they can't breathe, so they feel just like I did, like I had a slab of concrete on my chest, choking me to death. Then they make them inhale something that may not even make them better!

Discuss: Why are they both keen that their word is right?

2   There are many different organisations involved in the animals in medical research debate, each with a different viewpoint and each keen to convince the public to agree with their view.

Ask: Who do you think these groups are and what point of view would they have? (i.e. Animal Rights Groups – you might like to draw the distinction between extremists, activists and those who campaign for animal welfare, medical research organisations, drugs companies. Refer also to the Media and their interest in having an angle and story)

3   Read articles 1 (Animal Aid) and 2 (A mock up of a tabloid news article) from *Information Sheet: Articles*.

Discuss the following questions:

What words are used to describe: Scientists; Animal Rights Campaigners; Animals; Experiments; The outcomes of experiments; The behaviour of Animal Rights Campaigners?

- What phrases have the biggest impact on you? Why?
- What does the article focus on? What are its main themes?
- Does it tend to use facts or opinions? Does it seem to appeal more to reason or emotion?
- What impact does the article have on you?
- Do you think this is the aim of the piece?
- Does it present a balanced view?

4   Read articles 3 (A mock up of newspaper 'comment' piece) and 4 (A mock up of a broadsheet news article) from *Information Sheet: Articles* and discuss the same questions.

5   Is it possible to identify the source of each article from the list below at the bottom of the sheet?

6   Which articles do you trust the most? Why?

7   Use the information from all the articles on *Information Sheet: Articles* and what you have learned from the play to write your own piece.

Decide if it is going to be:

- emotive or objective
- For or Against or Neutral
- for a Tabloid or Broadsheet Newspaper or Campaign organisation

Give your article a headline, then write your article.

Information Sheet – Articles (English Lesson)

ARTICLE 1

Animal Experiments

Each year inside British laboratories, approximately three million animals are experimented on. Every 12 seconds, one animal dies. Cats, dogs, rats, mice, guinea pigs, rabbits, primates (monkeys) and other animals are used to test new products, to study human disease and in the development of new drugs – they are even used in warfare experiments.

Animal Aid opposes animal experiments on both moral and scientific grounds. Animals are not laboratory tools. They are sentient creatures capable of experiencing pain, fear, loneliness, frustration and sadness.

To imprison animals and deny them their freedom and ability to express natural instincts, to deliberately inflict pain, cause extreme suffering, mental distress, and ultimately a premature and often slow and protracted death all in the name of science is unacceptable. All the more so because the experiments are bad science in the first place: they do not work and have the potential to harm human health. Ending vivisection will benefit people as well as animals.

In January 2004 a landmark victory was won in the campaign against animal experiments. Cambridge University, which had for several years been planning to build a multi-million pound primate research centre, announced it was shelving the plans, following a public inquiry at which it was unable to back up its claims that the research to be carried out there would benefit human health. Hundreds of monkeys each year will now be spared the horror of confinement, torture and death inside a laboratory. Animal Aid is actively campaigning against a new animal laboratory under construction at Oxford University.

Every year, Animal Aid's Mad Science Awards highlight the ludicrous and horrific scientific research carried out on animals. The 2004 awards went to researchers at Oxford and Cambridge conducting experiments on monkeys.

ARTICLE 2

Arrests over medical research farm horror campaign

On Tuesday Police arrested five people as part of their probe into a long and violent campaign waged against the owners of a farm which bred guinea pigs for medical research.

The Ball family at Marosa Farm in Suffolk endured death threats, abuse, and in the worst incident of a six-year campaign, a family grave was desecrated.

The family said that in August the business would return to traditional farming, in the hope that it would lead to the return of the body of Christina Mills, mother-in-law of one of the co-owners.

Staffordshire detectives raided four addresses in the early hours of Tuesday morning, arresting a 37-year-old man in Leeds, a 35-year-old man in Warwick, a 39-year-old man in Sheffield and a 38-year-old woman in Woodbridge, Suffolk.

Arrests were made on suspicion of conspiracy to blackmail Darren Ball and Partners. Detectives had also arrested another woman, 25, in Sheffield on suspicion of obstructing police and on assaulting an officer.

The grave of Mills, who died seven years ago aged 81, was dug up and her remains taken in September 2003.

No group has yet claimed responsibility for the action, the culmination of one of the longest campaigns of harassment by animal rights activists in Britain today.

ARTICLE 3

Comment: Testing Times for the Animal Experimenters

So Darley Oaks – the so-called 'farm' in which guinea pigs were bred for experimental purposes – is to close down, in a momentous but all-too-rare success for the animal rights movement. As expected in a political environment where the animal-testing lobby holds all the cards, the media reaction has been one-sided, with airtime and newsprint given over to the angry mutterings of scientists acting as the mouthpieces of the pharmaceutical industry.

Such a unanimous chorus of outrage obscures the fact that an ever-increasing number of scientists and doctors oppose animal testing on purely practical grounds – because, simply put, it doesn't work, and it often makes things worse. This growing tendency among those brave enough to speak out has found an outlet in the group Europeans for Medical Progress. This independent, non-profit-making organisation, run by and for scientists and medical professionals, points out that tests on animals 'exhaust precious research funding, waste valuable time, produce ineffective solutions, and delay progress toward human cures'. Their argument is straightforward enough (which is perhaps all the excuse the nay-sayers need to pour scorn on it): that animals are too different, in both physiological and biological terms, to provide an accurate guide to how a drug is likely to act on humans. They point out the many superior alternatives to animal testing: in-vitro and population research, for instance, to say nothing of modern breakthroughs such as the DNA chip, computer modelling and micro-dose studies. At the same time, a statistical study has concluded that adverse drug reactions are the fourth highest cause of death in the Western world – in effect killing more people every year than die in traffic accidents.

A survey has shown that over eighty per cent of doctors mistrust animal testing, so why does it continue to have such a hold over the medical establishment? In a word, money. The industries that depend on these tests – manufacturers of cages and other instruments, breeders, and above all the pharmaceutical companies – have a vested interest in seeing them continue. And because the system is right at the heart of medical research, it is a great deal less trouble for scientists to produce papers that use animal testing for their results – thus gaining funding that much more quickly and easily. Equally, drugs that their companies want to rush out can use the long-established system of animal tests rather than looking for better, more reliable alternatives.

The results of such a reckless – and let's be clear, unscientific – approach were made very clear to everyone two years ago when the would-be wonder drug for arthritis, Vioxx, was shown to double the risk of a heart attack or stroke. Its makers, the vast multi-national Merck, now faces thousands of lawsuits, including one from the US-based Physicians Committee for Responsible Medicine, who argue that Merck decided to rely on tests showing that Vioxx was safe in mice, rats, and monkeys, while ignoring mounting evidence that the drug was dangerous to humans.

The soothing, media-friendly voices of the pro-testing lobby would no doubt poo-pooh any connection between the Vioxx disaster and the fate of the guinea pigs at Darley Oaks – while all the time, you can be sure, talking up the unrelated actions of a few angry extremists in the animal rights movement. But commonsense, and medical reasoning, suggest otherwise. Most experiments on guinea pigs concern research on skin irritation – research that, as the name suggests, causes the animal untold suffering – but because the skin of a guinea pig has a quite different physiological structure from that of a human, the tests barely tell us anything. It is in the interests of the testers to deprive us of any knowledge of this barbarous, pointless research, but the time will finally come when the niggling doubts people have about such testing – however much they are assured of its efficacy – will lead to greater public awareness and combine with the growing antagonism among experts, to consign animal experimentation to the dustbin of history, where it surely belongs.

ARTICLE 4

During the twentieth century, animal research acted as the catalyst for the majority of medical breakthroughs. In the UK, it is likely that the entire population has at some point benefited from anesthetics, vaccines and antibiotics, while those suffering from serious conditions have grown to rely upon treatments originally developed through animal research.

In recent years, research has also been used to explore possible treatments for more complex medical conditions such as heart disease, depression, AIDS and cancer. It is also often forgotten that advances in veterinary medicine have been as a direct result of animal research.

Scientists have worked to develop non-animal experimental methods which often help explain medical issues which animal studies would not be able to address. Despite efforts to reduce the use of animals in medical research, reviews of medical research continue to show the necessity of using animals for some experiments. Without animal experiments, there would be little hope for those suffering from serious conditions such as malaria, Alzheimer's disease, strokes, cystic fibrosis and spinal cord damage.

What are the alternatives?
The word 'alternative' suggests a choice between two or more options, and in the case of animal research, there really are no other options. If an in-vitro, non-animal method does become viable, then it would almost certainly be used. Currently, few in-vitro techniques can adequately replace the use of animals, with non-animal methods generally complementary rather than alternatives.

Lesson 8: IT
Presenting different points of view

Aim
To transfer information from video presentation to written document/power point presentation.

Objectives
To select relevant information from sources.

To organise and present information clearly and in a format appropriate to its audience.

National Curriculum Links
ICT: KS3 1b, 3a & 3b and KS4 1a, 3a & 3b

Resources
Access to weblink: **http://www.ytouring.org.uk/productions/breathe/education/moviemenu.html**

Activity
1   Explain the following background:

During the early stages of creating *Every Breath*, Y Touring Theatre Company invited a selection of speakers from different organisations involved in the use of animals in medical research debate to come to a workshop where they could present their point of view on the issues involved.

The videos of those talks are viewable on weblink: **http://www.ytouring. org.uk/productions/breathe/education/moviemenu.html**

2   Divide the class into small groups (i.e. two to four). Each group needs access to the internet. Assign each group a speaker from the list below:

- Antony Burn – British Union for Anti Vivisection
- Vickie Cowell – Patient's Voice for Medical Advance
- Kathy Archibald – Europeans for Medical Progress
- Ted Griffiths – Biomedical Research Educational Trust

Your task, in your groups, is to watch the video of the speaker's presentation and to communicate the point of view of that speaker and the organisation they represent to the rest of the group. This information can be communicated in one of the following ways:

- A written document. Copies could be produced for the class and the group could talk the class through the information contained in it
- Powerpoint presentation

The students could supplement the content of the videos by referring to:

- The introduction to speaker contained on their title page
- The website of the organisation they represent (see links on the speaker's title pages)

3   After allowing appropriate time for the students to prepare their
    presentations, ask each group to present their information.

    Discuss:

    - The relative strengths and weaknesses of each presentation
    - New things learnt about the animals in medical research debate

Y Touring Pulse Plays

Four downloadable plays for the schools education market. These plays cover a wide range of issues including disability, eugenics, sexuality, IVF, GM Foods and Genetics.

The texts include comprehensive background notes and suggested activities to introduce your group to the themes, context and underlying science explored in each.

Scenes from the Fair by Jonathan Hall
The summer of 1914 the future seems both bright and obvious, the new science of eugenics is the way forward. Fair Day 1918: has the bright shining new tomorrow won through despite the traumas of the past four years? (**F8 M10**)

Born of Glass by Rhiannon Tise
Four separate stories interweave as parents, and parents-to-be, strive for their ideal offspring, and a revolutionary game show is launched on television. The prize for the lucky winners? A new-born baby. (**F9 M7**)

Genes 'r' Us by Rahila Gupta
The year is 2040. Genetics is the new religion. The government of the day has been nurturing a generation of kids in a massive social engineering project. The first ever Pick-a-Gene day is being organised with all the fervour of a Pop Idol audition. (**F10 M8**)

Leap of Faith by Nicola Baldwin
The Iceman, Babyglider, X, Cat and their friends are 'Traceurs', free-running, making death-defying leaps and stunts across rooftops and. What makes you push yourself to the edge? Nature meets nurture, as the pattern of your genes threads a path through the pressures of your environment. (**F9 M9**)

These plays are available to download for a fee of £30 each.
Available through **www.oberonbooks.com** and **www.ytouring.org.uk**

ALSO AVAILABLE FROM OBERON BOOKS

Racism:

Colour of Justice
Edited by Richard Norton-Taylor   ISBN 1 84002 107 1   **£7.99**
In 1993, black teenager Stephen Lawrence was stabbed to death in a racist attack. Based on the transcripts of the public inquiry, this is a dramatic reconstruction of the hearings.

Gladiator Games
By Tanika Gupta   ISBN 1 84002 624 3   **£8.99**
Zahid Mubarek was murdered by his racist cellmate. Using a mixture of dramatisation and verbatim evidence, this play examines the way society treats young offenders and prison services and practices.

Silent Cry
By Madani Younis   ISBN 1 84002 507 7   **£7.99**
A death in police custody leads to an ordinary family looking for justice and tells the story of a mother's journey that begins as her son's life ends.

Health:

The Lemon Princess
By Rachael McGill   ISBN 1 84002 542 5   **£7.99**
Mike and his daughter Becky are close, working the Leeds pub circuit with a bickering stage double-act. Becky's behaviour becomes increasingly strange – the cause is CJD.

Plays for Young People
By Philip Osment   ISBN 1 84002 272 8   **£14.99**
Four plays dealing with issues of gender, AIDS, disability, relationships, ethnic strife, crime, drugs and bullying. Can young people caught up in self-destructive cycles break free?

Perpetua
By Fraser Grace   ISBN 1 84002 122 5   **£7.99**
The battle between May Lake abortion clinic and pro-lifers Operation Freedom pits the law of God against the law of the land and the right of life against the right to choose.

Burn / Rosalind
Two plays by Deborah Gearing   ISBN 1 84002 659 6   **£8.99**
Burn – Birdman. 15 years old, no family, no friends – a loner with nothing to lose. This powerful and inspiring play is a unique portrait of teenage life, drawn with startling and refreshing honesty.
Rosalind – The story of Rosalind Franklin and the discovery of the structure of DNA.

the siege
By Adrian Mitchell   ISBN 1 870259 67X   **£8.99**
An epic play, specifically for schools, which explores what happens when bigotry is exploited by politicians and how peaceful actions can result in a brighter future.

Available from all good bookshops or online at **www.oberonbooks.com**
info@oberonbooks.com   020 7607 3637